SOCIAL REALITIES
AND
COMMUNITY PSYCHIATRY

SOCIAL REALITIES
AND
COMMUNITY PSYCHIATRY

H. Warren Dunham

HUMAN SCIENCES PRESS
SUBSIDIARY OF BEHAVIORAL PUBLICATIONS INC.
72 FIFTH AVENUE, NEW YORK, N.Y. 10011

Library of Congress Catalog Number 74-10967

ISBN: 0-87705-215-8

BEHAVIORAL PUBLICATIONS, INC.
72 Fifth Avenue
New York, New York 10011

Printed in the United States of America
56789   987654321

Library of Congress Cataloging in Publication Data

Dunham, Henry Warren, 1906–
    Social realities and community psychiatry.

    Bibliography: p.
    1. Social psychiatry. 2. Psychiatric hospital care. 3. Mentally ill—
Rehabilitation. I. Title.
[DNLM: 1. Community mental health services. 2. Psychiatry, Commu-
nity. WM30 D917s]
RC455.D79   362.2'04'25   74-10967

Contents

List of Figures

Acknowledgments

I wish to express my gratitude to the following publishers for their permission to reprint three of the chapters included in this volume: Elsevier Publishing Company, Amsterdam, the Netherlands, for Chapter 3, "The Institutional Social Situation: Its Integrating Role in Psychiatric Therapy," first published in *Psychiatria, Neurologia, Neurochirurgia;* the *Archives of General Psychiatry* for Chapter 5, "Community Psychiatry: The Newest Therapeutic Bandwagon," and the F. A. Davis Company Publishers for Chapter 6, "Neglected Realities in the Development of Community Psychiatry."

I owe my special appreciation to Dr. Jacques Gottlieb, former director of Lafayette Clinic and chairman of the Department of Psychiatry, for his leadership in providing an environment at the Clinic that encouraged independent thought and research. Many of these articles were written under his clinic stewardship. I wish to express my thanks to Dr. Garfield Tourney, chairman of the Department of Psychiatry at Wayne State University, who critically reviewed the entire manuscript and is responsible for the Foreword. To Maxwell Jones, M.D. and Elaine Cumming, Ph.D. go my thanks for their critical Afterwords, which have enriched this volume.

I also extend my thanks to Dr. Elliot Luby and the late Dr. Peter Beckett for their critical reading of several of the included chapters. To Ernest Gruenberg, M.D., Morton Kramer, Sc.D., Bruce Dohrenwend, Ph.D., and Leo Srole, Ph.D. go my heartfelt thanks for the several conversations with each of them that have helped to clarify and, I hope, tighten some of the conceptions that I have expressed in this volume. Finally, I wish to thank Mrs. Barbara Srinivasen for her careful construction of the two charts contained in Chapter 4 and Mrs. Edna Moritz for her competent secretarial skills in preparing this volume for the press.

H. Warren Dunham
October 1, 1974

Foreword

Psychiatry is facing the criticism of a vast number of fault-finders at the present time, both from left-wing and right-wing organizations, and from certain moderate and realistic evaluations of our profession as well. What is known as psychiatry includes many divergent viewpoints that have been called a "babel of many voices." On the one hand the public has many magical expectations for what psychiatry can do in achieving a desired utopian state of hedonistic bliss, while on the other hand severe criticism continues for its inability to deal with many of the recurring problems of our society. Psychiatrists themselves have tended to expand their responsibilities to encompass all areas of human life and performance. The definition of psychiatric illness has greatly expanded, and the field seems to ride in all directions encompassing social, psychological, and many biological problems. Some psychiatrists claim with religious fervor to have a solution to many of the problems of society, while others are extremely conservative in their acknowledgment of any achievements within our field during the past 25 years.

Throughout the history of psychiatry, exposure to criticism has been by no means a unique phenomenon. Problems of poverty, criminality, chronic mental disorder, mental deficiency, convulsive disorders, and many other illnesses have fallen under the rubric of psychiatry. In Weir Mitchell's famous speech at the semicentennial of the American Medico-Psychological Association (now the American Psychiatric Association) in 1894, he emphasized the need for the psychiatrists to return to the field of medicine, to escape from the large isolated state institutions, and to carefully examine their accomplishments. Similar criticisms have been made by others over the years.

It is interesting to note that on the centennial anniversary of the birth of Sigmund Freud in 1956, at the annual meeting of the American Psychiatric Association, Ernest Jones spoke of Freud as initiating the "great psychiatric revolution" and said that psychoanalysis gives one a general theory of behavior encompassing psychopathology as well as behavior as a whole. Psychoanalysis was regarded not only as a form of psychiatric therapy, but as a science having widespread applicability in solving many of the problems of society. However, at the same meeting, the renowned neurologist and neurosurgeon Percival Bailey regarded this "great psychiatric revolution" as in many ways being a fiasco. He severely criticized psychoanalysis, emphasizing that analysts could demonstrate no statistical evidence that their therapeutic results were any greater than those of other forms of psychotherapy, that they had solved few problems, and that they had established a rabbinical tradition of education rather than one based upon laboratory experimentation. He noted the isolation of psychoanalysis from medicine and felt that all too often the analysts were working within their own "ivory tower" institutes and offices while neglecting the major problems of the psychoses and organic brain disorders.

Since 1956 a number of changes have occurred. We have seen the emergence of psychopharmacology and re-emphasis on biological methods in psychiatry. On the other hand we have seen an increasing social orientation toward many aspects of psychiatric problems. In 1961 the final report of the Joint Commission on Mental Illness and Health appeared in summary in the book *Action for Mental Health*. These recommendations for a national mental health program did much to stimulate the field of community psychiatry with attempts to better utilize manpower and establish mental health centers in which comprehensive care could be given to the mentally disturbed. The program aimed at the education of the general public, the acceptance and recognition of mental illness, and attempts to overcome the pervasive defeatism that often stands in the way of effective treatment. Community psychiatry in many ways separated itself from psychiatry as a medical discipline and came to exist as a social action movement largely influenced by public pressures, political forces, and legislative measures at the local, state, and federal levels. Its theoretical basis rested on the knowledge gained from the social and behavioral "sciences" rather than from the specialty of psychiatry within the discipline of medicine. The traditional doctor-patient relationship was often rejected, and a shift in diagnosis and therapy to the family and to the community took place. Meanwhile, modern conventional private psychiatric practice has often isolated itself from the general domain of medicine, in many ways just as hospital psychiatry isolated itself 80 years or so ago. Many of the results expected from community psychiatry and the private practice of the profession have not come to fruition and recently have again been exposed to considerable criticism.

A major issue in all these criticisms is the medical model versus the social model interpretation of mental illness. Is a mental illness comparable to a physical disease? Is there a constellation of symptoms and signs that we can diagnose as a type of illness that follows a particular course, that has a particular pattern of psychopathology as well as possible physical pathology, and is responsive to medical modes of treatment, such as the utilization of drugs, physical methods of therapy, and psychotherapy? Or, on the other hand, is what is designated as mental illness a social prejudice reflecting the attitudes of our society and its many problems as they affect the individual? Some psychiatrists, such as Laing, have completely rejected the concept of schizophrenia as a psychiatric disorder that should be treated along medical and psychotherapeutic lines. Laing regards the society as being "schizophrenic" and the "patient" himself as being essentially normal. It is the aim of these individuals following the social model to alter the structure of society and, in so doing, to eliminate mental illness. In many ways, this is an age-old idea best exemplified by Rousseau's interpretation of society in the 18th century and in Karl Marx's criticism of capitalism in the 19th century as being causative for the many ills of mankind.

There have also been numerous attacks on psychotherapy. Questions have been raised, such as Eysenck's devastating criticism, as to the validity of psychotherapy. Eysenck has emphasized that comparisons of treated patients with untreated control subjects show that the results of psychoanalysis are minimal, if they exist at all. However, with the attack on psychotherapy there has come about a vogue for many different types of psychotherapies. We are in a phase of "therapeutic enthusiasm" and crazes. Many types of individual therapy and group therapy exist with little basis in fact, and for which there are no clear-cut follow up or comparative studies. Often they revolve around a charismatic figure who has a strong following and too often exploits the following for his own personal economic and egotistical gain. Such therapies are presented with tremendous enthusiasm and claim great results, but they are never carefully studied and evaluated.

During the past 25 years there have been rapid changes in our society and culture. War has been an almost constant phenomenon. There has been a great explosion in terms of our knowledge. Over-population and ecological issues have reached the forefront of man's problems. With these changes there has also been a disorganization of the family unit, with increases in the rates of divorce and illegitimacy. We have shifted from belief in a Protestant work ethic as a goal for the citizen to a largely pleasure-oriented, hedonistic way of life. To some extent, psychiatry has played a role in these changes. Certainly many of the patterns of permissiveness in child rearing and certain aspects of the breakdown of the family unit have been readily accepted and even promoted by a number of psychiatrists. However, there are a great number of vast changes within the society that are beyond the control or fault of psychiatrists. Such changes are very difficult to predict and to control in any systematic way.

These papers of the distinguished social scientist and epidemiologist of mental disorder, H. Warren Dunham, do much to clarify these problems as they have emerged in the field of psychiatry during the past 25 years. Professor Dunham has been well recognized as one of the major pioneers in the discipline that we now call "social psychiatry." His early work with R. E. L. Faris, *Mental Disorders in Urban Areas,* appeared in 1939. This proved to be a great stimulus for much later work by investigators into the role of social factors in the cause and course of mental disorders.

Professor Dunham has pursued his initial interests in a number of ways, re-examining and restudying his own data, as well as extending his methods and collecting further data to clarify and modify some of his original findings. For example, although in his study of 1939 with Faris he postulated a causal mechanism between social class and schizophrenia (schizophrenia having a greater prevalence in the lower classes), he later modified his views in interpretating the phenomena observed as a matter of social selection occurring with the progression of the illness. Such alterations in his views with the presentation of new data were well revealed in his book *Community and Schizophrenia,* which appeared in 1965, and in some papers of the period presented here. Many aspects of psychiatry have been exposed to his careful and objective vision. His orientation as a social scientist has been that of an observer rather than of one striving to change the field of psychiatry with the proclamation of new social therapeutic triumphs. Although a critic of many aspects of psychiatry, Dunham never succumbs to the tenets of the antipsychiatry movement which has gained popularity among some segments of the social sciences, legal profession, and general populace. He aims at the clarification of the field, the patterns of care, and the role of social factors in mental disorder. Furthermore, he points out the many limitations of the field and the need to return to "hard" data in the area of therapeutic modalities, treatment results, the patterns of both hospital and community care, and the recent developments in early discharge and aftercare methods.

Another great therapeutic revolution, community psychiatry, with its many innovations, in many ways becomes a mirage of our illusory thinking. The medical model for psychiatric disorder is not rejected, but clarified, as Professor Dunham delineates the differences between mental diseases, which often have a biologic basis, and psychological adjustment problems, which reflect the family and cultural organization of the society.

Dunham's studies on community psychiatry have been most thought provoking, and have already been widely discussed and admired by many psychiatrists and social scientists. It is refreshing to examine the views of a tough-minded thinker, rather than a tender-minded existential romanticist, as he attempts to objectively study the data, or lack of data, in our field, along with the many current movements in treatment and theory.

Garfield Tourney, M.D.
Dept. of Psychiatry
Wayne State U. School of Medicine

Author's Preface

A book is a very personal thing. For despite an objective style, it is closely connected with the personal experiences of the author. So it is with these papers in which I attempt to take a critical look at the development of selected social programs and policies that have been concerned with abetting the recovery of those persons who have been regarded by psychiatrists or members of the community as mentally ill.

The prevailing uncertainty and vagueness of our knowledge concerning the causes of most mental diseases have made the therapeutic task in psychiatry a most dubious and discouraging procedure. This is reflected in the faddish quality of many types of psychiatric therapy and the tendency for one therapeutic fad to die out as soon as another one puts in an appearance. Thus, within the past fifty years psychi-

15

atric therapy has ranged from proposals for educating attendants about mental illness to occupational therapy, hydrotherapy, chemotherapy, shock therapy (both electric and insulin), lobotomies, long psychoanalysis, short psychoanalysis, indirect psychotherapy, direct psychotherapy, music therapy, group therapy, pharmaceutics, therapeutic milieus, night hospitals, day hospitals, community mental health centers and encounter groups. It would seem to be quite clear that some of these therapies are medical, others are psychological, and still others are sociological. The succession of therapies over the years is in part a response to the frustration experienced by psychiatrists because of the paucity of therapeutic successes.

I have focused my attention in these chapters upon four psychiatric therapeutic programs which span the past twenty years. My critiques of these programs rest upon the following assumptions:

(1) That the psychoses are diseases and, following the medical model, individuals who have these diseases are qualitatively different from those who do not.

(2) That the various neurotic reactions and behavior deviations are emotional disturbances or learned patterns of the personality and when these reactions and deviations are described and measured in a sample of people from a given culture they tend to form a normal probability continuum.

(3) That the culture of a group influences and shapes the content but not the form of the psychoses.
(4) That culture by means of the socialization process shapes and organizes the personality structure.
(5) That some psychoses and some mental deficiencies have a genetic foundation.
(6) That much therapy at the present time, especially with regard to the psychoses, is a matter of trial and error and a search for a social niche in the community into which a given patient can be fitted.
(7) That mental diseases are to be distinguished from psychological adjustment problems and learned deviant behavior both of which are culturally grounded. Thus, psychological adjustment problems and deviant behaviors are not mental diseases even though they may require various rehabilitative and corrective types of programs for their alleviation.

My first concern with these several programs is an analysis of the therapeutic milieu as an effective device for the recovery of psychiatric patients. Chapter 2 was written early in 1956 and is a development of my reaction to the experiences provided by the "Conference of Socio-Environmental Aspects of Treatment of Patients in Mental Hospitals" which convened in Boston sometime in the late spring of

1955. I had in the previous year reviewed Maxwell Jones's *The Therapeutic Community*[1] and found in it a reinforcement of an older notion that I had developed when I began my epidemiological studies in Chicago, namely, that the state hospital should be studied as an institution from a cultural point of view. I subsequently met Dr. Jones at the Conference and was further intrigued by the type of program that he had developed at Belmont Hospital.

At the time I had also finished my own study[2] on the culture of the state mental hospital and this was perhaps the most crucial experience that led to the concern I have expressed in Chapter 2. My intention here was merely to raise a question about the significance of the therapeutic community in relation to recovery and to require some hard evidence as to its effectiveness. As I began to look at the various programs of this nature that were being initiated in some of the hospitals throughout the country, I developed a certain skepticism regarding the enthusiasm often engendered among some professionals in support of them. I could not but see the therapeutic milieu as a linear descendant of moral treatment that had emerged in Europe and had been transmitted to the United States in the early part of the nineteenth century, of programs inaugurated later in the nineteenth century emphasizing the training of attendants, of the therapeutic endeavors of L. C. Marsh at Worcester State Hospital in the early 1930s[3] with his aphorism, "By the group you have been broken, by the group you will be healed," and by the "Total Push" therapy suggested by the late Abraham Myerson.[4] With these previous programs as background, now comes the therapeutic milieu of the fifties which was to usher in another psychiatric renaissance.

In a like fashion the analysis contained in Chapter 3 was a direct result of spending an academic year (1956-1957) in Europe, where I had the opportunity to visit several state hospitals in Norway, England and the Netherlands. It seemed to me at the time that the superintendents of these European mental hospitals were attempting to break new ground and to shake up the traditional culture that had encompassed these hospitals in the past. I viewed what was happening in these institutions as an attempt to construct a new hospital culture that would bring together the various therapies and thus enable all of their proponents to work together as a team in an effort to cure the patient.

There is no question that the time was ripe for accepting and initiating these ideas about reshaping the traditional hospital culture, and they were received enthusiastically by many psychiatrists and social scientists. This enthusiasm is shown most forcefully in Goodwin Watson's "Foreword" to *The Therapeutic Community*, where he proclaims:

> Psychiatry now verges upon another great forward step, one which may have consequences even more far reaching than those flowing from psychoanalytic discoveries. In the field of mental health, most attention has been given to psychotherapy; some to mental hygiene, *but very*

little as yet to the design of a whole culture that
will foster healthy personalities. [5] (Italics mine)

The next four papers were written between the
years of 1964 and 1968 and in a sense are by-products
of my epidemiological study of schizophrenia. In
some quarters they were regarded as a bucket of cold
water thrown on the expectations that the new community mental health movement had engendered.
Right on the heels of the emergence of community
psychiatry came the "me too" boys—community
medicine, community psychology and community
social work—all wanting to be cut in on the action.

The research-clinic setting of my epidemiological research provided me with an intimate glimpse
of the current diagnostic and therapeutic practices of
psychiatry, contributing to the critical perspective of
these papers. I had already become aware in the
early fifties of the shortage of board-certified psychiatrists in the state hospitals as the younger psychiatrists fled to office practice made possible and
attractive by psychoanalysis, shock therapy and the
new pharmaceuticals. I was also observing from my
epidemiological post the widening definition of mental illness as the psychiatric net became more and
more extended.[6] This widening definition of mental
illness appears to be in part a response to the increased pressures for conformity developing in
American society during the fifties[7] and in part a
response to the frustrations in therapeutic results experienced by practicing psychiatrists.[8] It seemed to
me that the quick acceptance of the ideas embodied

in the new community psychiatry often seemed to represent a denial of the solid scientific contributions that researchers in psychiatry had made in the course of its history.

My attempt at a theoretical analysis of some of the social consequences of the early-release policy for schizophrenics had been brewing for some time and came to fruition when Dr. Marvin Herz of the Department of Psychiatry at Columbia University asked me to take part in a panel devoted to this policy. It seemed to me that there was a touch of magical thinking in the policy, for it seemed to indicate that because the hospital stay of schizophrenics was becoming shorter and shorter, this was a sign that schizophrenics were being successfully treated. At first, no one really raised the question, What were the social conditions under which the discharged schizophrenics were living in the community? The hospitals preferred to say to the public, "Look what a good job your mental hospitals are doing." The former question is now being heard more often and a more careful evaluation of these accumulated experiences may help to develop a policy that provides improved therapy for the patient and more adequate protection for the family and community.

Several themes are touched on often in this book. One theme emphasizes that the family and community are continually in a process of change and the psychiatric formulations do not sufficiently recognize this fact and so present a picture of family and community that is very much out of date. In fact, it might be said that community in the sense of a core of common values, mutual interdependence and respect and the acceptance of status differences in our society has practically disappeared. Another theme implicit here is the clear recognition of the necessity to formulate and implement a mental health policy that is based on current existing knowledge of etiology, prevention, therapy and rehabilitation with respect to mental illness. It would seem that achievement of a more adequate balance in this matter would represent a contribution to the maintenance of social order. Still another implicit theme suggests that a careful adherence to the medical model enables the psychiatrist to escape from being utilized as an agent of social control by social forces of which he is unaware. Thus, he has to make in his diagnoses clearcut distinctions between mental illness, psychological adjustment problems and culturally based deviant behavior even though in reality these conditions are not entirely unrelated.

It is hoped that these papers will lead to a more realistic appraisal of the therapeutic possibilities on the part of mental health professionals. Perhaps they can also point to those mental health policies that are humane with respect to the patient and balanced with respect to our culture.

REFERENCES

1. *American Sociological Review,* Vol. XIX, (June, 1954) 359–360.

2. Dunham, H. Warren and Weinberg, S. Kirson, *The Culture of the State Mental Hospital*, (Detroit: Wayne State University Press, 1960).
3. Marsh, L. C., "An Experiment in the Group Treatment of Patients at the Worcester State Hospital," *Mental Hygiene*, 1933, 17, 396–416.
4. Myerson, Abraham, "Theory and Principles of the 'Total Push' Method in the Treatment of Chronic Schizophrenia," *American Journal of Psychiatry*, 1939: 95, 1197–1204.
5. New York: Basic Books, Inc., 1953, p. VII.
6. Menninger, W. C., *Psychiatry in a Troubled World*, (New York: The Macmillan Company, 1948).
7. Reisman, David, *The Lonely Crowd*, (New Haven, Connecticut, Yale University Press, 1950).
8. Halleck, S. L., *The Politics of Therapy*, (New York: Science House, Inc., 1971); see also Schofield, W., *Psychotherapy: The Purchase of Friendship*, (Englewood Cliffs, New Jersey, Prentice-Hall, Inc., 1964).

—1—

An Introduction:
Ambivalence in Mental Health

This book deals with an era of psychiatry which emerged in the early 1950s when new insights, new ideas, new programs and new imaginative orientations struggled for recognition. Some eight years after World War II, the education, training and research programs in psychiatry and allied professions financed by the federal government began to make their contributions to the knowledge, treatment and prevention of mental disorders. It also was a time when numerous international bodies were formed with the intention of turning our psychiatric renaissance into an international one.

The psychiatric programs considered in this book are a reflection of our *Zeitgeist* which emphasizes that social conditions, interpersonal stress and

economic insecurity account for mental maladjustments and even certain psychotic conditions. If these
assumptions are true, concerned psychiatrists must
focus their energies on those very conditions which
tend to disorganize and possibly disintegrate the
mind of man. If the assumptions are false, the current
direction of psychiatry in America makes no sense,
and we have simply wasted our time and energy in
trying to make an impact upon the inevitable.

The national *Zeitgeist*, however, is itself a reflection of the deeply embedded belief that man
becomes what he is because of the obstacles which
confront him and the pathological situations which
surround him. The therapeutic goal is to change
these obstacles and pathological situations. This
stance is most western. By placing the burden of
man's lot upon the world and not upon himself, it
stands in sharp contrast to the philosophy of the East
which stresses the necessity of mastering one's impulsive life and irrational urges in order to control
the world. The viewpoint of the East is seen clearly
in the notion that man poses, but God disposes; while
in the West the notion is prevalent that God poses
and man disposes. President Kennedy reflected this
Western position clearly in the concluding statement
of his inaugural address when he said "that God's
work on earth must truly be our own."

While I am a product of this Western viewpoint
I am also critical of it. I suggest in this work that
before we act hastily and commit all our limited resources to any program promising significant therapeutic results for the mentally ill, we should take a

careful look at the implications and possible consequences of the program.

Thus, in Chapters 2 and 3, I take a critical look at the notion that a type of sociocultural environment can be created within the hospital that will be therapeutically advantageous to the patient. This idea has been developed from the British experience, particularly in the work of Maxwell Jones,[1] and has been supported by the several sociological studies that have examined the collective life of the mental hospital.[2] I suggest that the development of such a cultural climate in the hospital will contribute to a building of an improved morale in the staff. This improved staff morale would in all likelihood benefit the patient by providing a higher quality of care although it would by no means insure his recovery.

It is often argued that such an endeavor would tend to bring the climate of the mental hospital in line with the democratic character of the other institutions of American society. There are, of course, limitations. How far, for example, can democratic practices be extended to patients who need, in the light of their illness, authoritarian procedures? With respect to the hospital staff, however, where each staff member is constantly comparing his situation with democratic ethos of other social institutions, the endeavor seems highly desirable.

The next four chapters attempt a critical examination of the emerging field of community psychiatry. The mental health center and community psychiatry chapters began to take shape as I literally waded through an avalanche of memos, advertise-

ments, propaganda and articles dealing with some
real or imagined relationship between the community and mental health. All seemed to predict a psychiatric renaissance if psychiatry with its psychiatric
team would but turn its attention away from a preoccupation with the woes and anxiety of the individual
patient and begin to pay attention to the context of
community life in which the patient was inextricably
embedded. Working through this mountain of literature, I could not but wonder if the architects of this
new psychiatric specialty were not promising much
more than they could ever deliver.

As a sociologist I could hardly escape the thought
that the social scientists had done well in making
their impact upon psychiatry. For sociology as a discipline took, for one of its specialities, community organization. And here was a field of medicine literally
begging that the role of the community as a contributing agent in the development of mental maladjustments be recognized. Then, too, the federal
government got into the act, stimulated by the late
President Kennedy's 1963 address[3] which contributed to the making of funds available to the communities for new mental health programs. With
these new funds soon made available, ideas and programs began to multiply. This was a case of ideas
following money rather than the case of money following ideas.

In Chapter 4 I try to draw a distinction between
the new subfield of community psychiatry and the
development of community mental health centers.
The idea of such a center, which has taken shape in

many countries of the Western world, is sound and, of course, tends to bring together all of the available therapeutic devices that are operative in the mental health field and at the same time maintain a continuity of care for the patient. Here also the sailing is not clear, and I merely attempt to catalogue some of the difficulties in the development of such therapeutically effective centers.

Community psychiatry (Chapter 5), in contrast, implies almost a total reorganization of psychiatric ideology directed toward the notion that in the network of community relationships there is to be found the ingredients for the development of those types of maladjustments which eventually become labeled as mental disorders. All that was attempted here was to emphasize the necessity of proceeding cautiously by pointing to the confusion among psychiatrists as to what constituted community psychiatry, by making explicit the etiological assumptions underlying this new specialty and finally, by indicating that there was a tremendous complexity, unrecognized by its advocates, in turning to a treatment of the community as a means for maximizing the mental health of populations.

In Chapter 6 I attempt to indicate that certain established facts and knowledge concerning mental illness stand in the way and literally block the road to the development of a comprehensive community psychiatry. In addition, I try to point out the anxieties and the confusion that will grip the psychiatrist as he moves into that shaky terrain which constitutes the organization of the community. For here indeed is the real world, in fact a real world that the psychiatrist never made, or even thought of in his wildest dreams as he moved through school, the university and his residency training. While additional residency training might help to bring the psychiatric resident closer to this world, nevertheless, such training would still be too short for him ever to feel that he is on solid ground.

Chapter 7 asks the question, Where is community psychiatry going? Here I attempt to drive home in as sharp a fashion as possible the implications found in community psychiatry. These implications embody (1) a specific view of what constitutes community organization, (2) a view of the community in terms of its role as a causative agent of mental maladjustment and (3) the notion that there is some ideal form of community life that will be conducive to mental health rather than mental illness. These implications are discussed and are ever present in any consideration of the nature of community psychiatry. And above all, the intention is to question their validity. And if their validity is not sound or does not rest upon an accepted body of evidence the entire structure will come crumbling down.

This new emphasis on the role of community both as a treatment center and an etiological force points to the necessity of examining the recent policy of the early release of mental patients from the old custodial state hospitals. This I attempt in Chapter 8. While the focus in this chapter is primarily upon the schizophrenic patient, much of what has been hypothesized would apply to mental patients in general. Here the emphàsis is on the discrepancy of the fit between the needs of the mental patient and the reality of current family and community life. The consequences of this situation are derived and analyzed.

In Chapter 9, I take up a pressing issue that confronts any person or group that attempts to formulate social policy in a particular area. Here we always have the intention of basing our social policies on what validated knowledge we possess. But, if our knowledge is deficient, we should at least try to anticipate what it will be. For action is always necessary and man must act in order to live and how he acts and the manner in which he does it will not wait upon the development of new knowledge. But as knowledge advances, it is our hope that our policy will become more rational and organized in such a fashion that the ends which we seek will be obtained.

Finally, in Chapter 10 I show the various ways in which these new, recent programs for coping with mental disorders can provide the experiences for the development of more adequate therapeutic and preventive devices in the future. We must continue to align our hopes, our dreams and our humanitarianism with the scientific knowledge that we have accumulated concerning mental illness. While we can continue to move toward a goal of a high level of physical and mental health for all our people, we at the same time must realize that this constitutes an ideal and that persons have to learn to accept their ailments and to cope with them in some way. The development of a social policy in the mental health area that takes into account our existing scientific knowledge as well as our past experiences should be a contribution to a more successful coping with mental disorders.

REFERENCES

1. *The Therapeutic Community: A New Treatment Method in Psychiatry* (New York: Basic Books, 1953).
2. See A. Stanton and M. Schwartz, *The Mental Hospital: A Study of Institutional Participation in Psychiatric Illness and Treatment* (New York: Basic Books, 1953); I. Belknap, *Human Problems of a State Mental Hospital,* (New York: McGraw-Hill, 1956); W. Caudill, *The Psychiatric Hospital As a Small Society* (Cambridge, Massachusetts: Harvard University Press, 1958); H. W. Dunham and S. K. Weinberg, *The Culture of the State Mental Hospital* (Detroit: Wayne State University Press, 1960).
3. J. F. Kennedy, "Message from the President of the United States Relative to Mental Illness and Mental Retardation," *American Journal of Psychiatry,* 120 (February, 1964): 729–737.

—2—

The Culture of the State Mental Hospital: Is It of Therapeutic Significance?

The attempt to conceptualize the culture of the state mental hospital is illustrative of that body of sociological theory concerned with the organization and functioning of institutional subcultures. Thus, the culture of the school, factory, prison, business organization or governmental bureau should, as far as theory is concerned, be related to the analysis of the culture of the mental hospital. But, in addition to this theoretical concern, there is also an immediate practical value to be served in bringing to a level of conscious awareness the character of mental hospital culture.

Read at Annual Meeting of Society for the Study of Social Problems, September 1956, Detroit, Michigan.

This value is reflected in the following question: What significance, if any, does the hospital culture have in impeding or facilitating the therapy and recovery of patients? More tentatively, one might ask, Does the culture of the hospital have any significance with respect to therapy and recovery of patients? If it does, what is its significance? For our original question implied that the hospital culture might, in certain cases, impede therapy and, in other cases, facilitate it. Or a given hospital culture might contain both impeding and facilitating ingredients with respect to therapy and recovery. Under the assumption that hospital culture and therapeutic outcome are related, it should be theoretically possible—we only need empirical accounts of a representative sample of state hospital cultures—to arrange hospital cultures along a continuum from that one which most impeded to that which most facilitated therapy. But lacking such knowledge of a sample of hospital cultures, we must proceed more modestly and attempt to examine the problem within the confines of our present knowledge concerning mental-hospital culture. Thus, as a focus here I would like to suggest the following hypothesis: that state mental hospital culture which in its structure and functioning is farthest removed from the culture of other institutions functioning in the community will be most impeding with respect to the therapy and recovery of patients.

This hypothesis implies, of course, that the culture of the state mental hospital has been and will continue to be, unless something is done about it, at a marked variance to the culture of other institutions in the community and this proposition has been documented by numerous observations. Consequently, I am attempting the following four tasks:

(1) To depict in ideal-type form some of the chief characteristics of state mental hospital culture.
(2) To analyze hospital practices and cultural forms which have been recognized as related to patient behavior and therapy.
(3) To consider hospital culture in the light of general social change, and
(4) To examine some possibilities for a restructuring of mental hospital culture that will maximize the probability of returning the patient to his family and community.

The culture of the state mental hospital, like the culture of other institutions in our society, must be viewed as a product of a long evolutionary development. The specific cultural forms, as we abstract and depict them in the present, for most state hospitals are the resultants of the interactions in and between many generations of hospital life. But these resultants are also dynamic in that they provide clues to the emergent changes. We do not intend here to sort out all of the influences that have entered and converged into making the culture of the state hospital what it is today, but merely to indicate that some of these influences were European importations and others resulted from certain elements peculiar to the American cultural scene.

One aspect of the European influence deserves mention here, for it provided an ideology of state hospital practice in the first state hospitals in the United States founded in the first decade of the nineteenth century. Pinel in France and Tuke in England had been introducing a humane type of treatment for the mentally ill which geared the entire hospital to a concern with patient welfare. This procedure came to be known as "moral treatment" and replaced much of the previous reliance upon strictly medical therapies. The reported successes of "moral treatment" fired the imagination of many hospital superintendents and so set the stage for the introduction of this form of treatment into the first established state hospital in this country. The significance of this new treatment was that it related the possibility of cure to the total administration of the hospital, starting with the selection of a superintendent who could grasp this relationship.

However, the hope inspired by this vision was soon to be dissipated. The lack of knowledge about the insane among the public, the lethargy of the medical profession, the general demand for parsimonious state administration, the growth of population and the turbulent development of the nineteenth-century economy—all contributed to pushing the state hospital into the background and leaving its administration too often to the unconcerned. The gradual separation of business from medical administration helped further to make it impossible for the hospital to be concerned with its major task: the curing of patients.

Another of these early influences which served to set the mold for the culture of the state hospital as it developed in the United States, was the wide gap in attitudes between the medical professionals and the general population concerning the nature of mental illness. The fears, anxieties and uncertainties about mental disturbances existing among the people of any community produced the demand that the people be protected from all possible contact with the generally recognized unpredictable behavior of the mentally ill. Hence, the attempt to protect the community became a basic issue as state hospitals were gradually established in this new country and their establishment speeded up by the reformative zeal of Dorothy Dix in the last half of the nineteenth century. Even in this latter movement the appeal played upon the humanitarian values that characterized the American culture rather than upon a rationalistic approach to the solution of problems.

What I am attempting to indicate is that the culture of the mental hospital as we examine it in our own day is explainable and understandable, like all of our social institutions, only when it is viewed in the historical context of the evolving cultural pattern and the specific conditions which characterized American life. Thus, both the location and the size of state mental hospitals were determined by the

American culture pattern and provided, in part, the foundation from which the cultural organization, as we see it today, was to emerge.

Its location, as a rule, was on the outskirts of a community—although sometimes the community expanded and tended to envelop it—so placed because of the need for the community to be protected from the insane and because of the stigma attached to mental illness. Thus, the anxieties and fears of people in the community, focused on the mental hospital at the outskirts, were productive frequently of an alienation that grew up between the personnel in the hospital and the people in the community. This resulted in the hospital's developing a social and cultural system relatively independent of influences from community institutions. Thus, it literally cut itself off from those influences which acted on the other institutions and brought about changes in them. Its major tie with the community was rather a formal one: a form of economic and political control of costs and staff recruitment stemming from some department of state government. This location and isolation of the state hospital from the community was further strengthened by requiring duty personnel, utility workers and professional staff to live in the institution as a part of salary—a practice geared to reducing the economic cost of the institution to the taxpayers.

The large size of the state hospital as measured by patient population served not only to abet the emergence of its own distinctive social and cultural system but also to tighten its alienation from the community. Again its growth in size was a reflection of the somewhat confused view that it was necessary to keep the costs of such institutions at a minimum. Indeed, we are not far removed from the often observed tendency in state systems to measure the effectiveness of a superintendent by his ability to reduce the per-patient-day cost rather than what should have been his goal: increasing the patient discharge and recovery rate. This measure of effectiveness was also a part of a general view found among both hospital personnel and other citizens that the only thing that could be done for the "insane" was to give them good custodian care—and if a superintendent began to get this care for a minimum cost, he might well expect the care to become more brutal. It reminds me of the remark of an old attendant to a newcomer to the wards, "listen boy, you are new here; never speak to a patient except to tell him what to do; leave them alone."[1]

As the state hospital evolved on the American scene its gradual isolation from the community enabled it to develop cultural forms which might be described as putting it more and more out of step with the culture of other institutions in the community. The rigidity of its cultural forms became more and more assured and the atmosphere generated by this isolation and rigidity was one of fear and suspicion.

Thus, conditioned by isolation, size and a Protestant concern for economy, the average state hospital has developed a dual cultural system. On the one hand there is the culture of the duty personnel containing various conditions, customs and practices which are designed to bring about the control and care of patients. On the other hand there is the culture of the patient group containing customs and practices which function to protect the patients from the more sordid and brutal devices imbedded in the culture of the duty personnel.

This dual system comprising the culture of the patient body and the culture of the attendant group is the key to an understanding of the state mental hospital. For the patients their status is defined not only in legal terms but also in the expectations of the attendant group. Thus, within mental hospital society there is no means of distinguishing a "normal" response from a psychotic one. All behavior of patients is regarded as being related to, or as an outcome, of their mental disorders.

Professional staff members also have their defined statuses although their roles frequently become uncertain and ambiguous. For they are placed in the position of literally having to fight the attendant both to get at the patient and to see that their orders are carried out. The doctors who entered the hospital with enthusiasm to try the therapeutic tools that they possess find their enthusiasm dampened as they begin to have experience with the numerous phases of attendant culture. They have three courses open to them. They fight it for a while generally without support from above and then resign. Or they accept the ambiguous definition of their roles and allow themselves to internalize the hospital culture. Or they withdraw with their values intact and devote themselves to bureaucratic paper work or their own research concerns.

The rigidity of the class lines in the hospital—of doctors, clerical workers and attendants—functions not only to maintain the cultural system but also to make line communication difficult. This produces poor definition of various roles, misunderstandings about therapy and tightening of the attendant culture.

In considering the attendant and patient culture, the role of the doctor and the class hierarchy in hospital society, we have only touched on a few of the elements that are pertinent in attempting to depict the cultural system of the state hospital. The most significant aspect of this culture is that it sets itself against any changes and sabotages the effort of the professionals who supposedly know some of the things that should be done if patients are to get well.

Now, having attempted to present in an ideal-type form some of the significant features of state hospital culture as we know it in our day, I wish to call attention to some of these features which both affect patient behavior and therapeutic goals. However, it is essential to distinguish those aspects of the hospital culture which engender patients' behavior responses from those aspects which are destructive of therapeutic procedures. For example, when J. D. Frank[2] reports, as he did in a recent study, that changes in the top administration of the hospital were registered by patients in terms of mounting tension and of an increase in disturbed behavior, we are forced to raise the question whether such changes in behavior are of significance in relation to eventual recovery. We regard psychic tension as unhealthy; we disapprove of disturbed behavior and approve of controlled behavior. The appearance of such behavior interferes with ward management. But does it interfere with eventual recovery? Likewise, when M. S. Schwartz[3] and A. H. Stanton isolated certain types of social situations on the ward that were productive of incontinence in three female patients, does this prolong eventual recovery? Again, of course, we want to control such unpleasant behavior in terms of ward management for if we do, perhaps more time will be given to such patients for other therapies. But other therapies will also be carried on, we assume, during the incontinent periods. What I have been attempting to point out here is that patients, like staff personnel, are a part of the total hospital as a sociocultural situation, and they will respond to certain elements in this situation, as staff personnel do, in ways that they have previously learned to respond or with defenses that they have acquired for their own ego protection.

There has been some consideration given recently in the literature to the types of attitudes among hospital personnel that are therapeutically advantageous to patients. But such attitudes are likely to be little manifest in the average state hospital until the punitive-controlling traditions for dealing with patients, so deeply embedded in the attendant culture, can be broken up. Consequently, it becomes necessary, instead of piously pointing to the desirable therapeutic attitude, to examine the hospital on a broad cultural canvas concerning dominant patterns of morale, of role and role conceptions of the leading professionals, particularly the superintendent. For these elements form the cultural matrix in which various attitudes, both therapeutic and otherwise, will be manifested.

Let us consider for a moment the issues involved in the authoritarian versus the democratic organization of the state hospital. This issue has come into focus largely because of the increasing democratization of other institutions of our culture while the state hospital continues in its more traditional authoritarian pattern. The often expressed belief that a more democratic hospital social structure will be of greater therapeutic value for patients may not in itself be true. But there are sound sociological reasons, as our hypothesis attests, for asserting that an authoritarian hospital social structure will have a deleterious affect on patients and personnel alike if it is functioning in a cultural situation where the other social institutions are democratically structured. This great chasm between the organization of the state hospital and other social institutions in the community accounts, in part, for the general feeling that the more democratic structure will lead to better therapeutic results. Staff interdiscipline conferences, sharing in decisionmaking, training programs for attendants and developing more and better rewards for all personnel are some of the devices that have been often advocated, and less often put into practice, for achieving a greater democratization and a high level of morale. But the traditional hospital culture has manifested its tenacity, as any culture will do, by fighting off such proposed changes with a resulting increase of frustration and discouragement by those members of the professional staff who have not internalized the hospital culture.

It may be true that persons not trained for change are most likely to fight it. In one state hospital system, where the eight-hour day for attendants was inaugurated some dozen years ago, there were some attendants used to the old twelve hours that protested the change. The very interesting experience of introducing patient government[4] at the Boston Psychopathic Hospital demonstrated its therapeutic value for patients, but not without complaints from the "old guard."

The roles and role conceptions held and maintained by the hospital professionals, particularly the superintendent, become of prime relevance in shaping the cultural climate of the hospital. The superintendent, the chief medical man, is the key person here, for if his own convictions concerning the function of a mental hospital, the disorders of the patients and the necessary therapeutic devices have not matured by the time he assumes his post, he will merely enter the ranks of that long list of hospital superintendents who have succumbed to and incorporated the hospital culture as they have found it, rather than becoming the agent for challenging it. But those superintendents that were not afraid and knew that the creative man is often a lonely man, succeeded in temporarily disorganizing the traditional hospital culture until it was permitted to slip back into its original mold by superintendents who followed such disturbers of the status quo. Such a role, in the traditional hospital culture, was not conducive to popularity, and any superintendent filling such a role was forced to make many compromises in order to maintain the institution as a going concern.

It would be expected that our state hospital system as part of our total culture would be responsive to changes taking place in the overall cultural organization. The great social and economic changes of the past fifty years have, however, made little impact on the state hospital as a cultural system. Even new developments in medical and psychological technology were slowly incorporated but with little noticeable impact upon the nonmaterial hospital culture. For it is our thesis that the cultural forms of the state hospital had become so set and hardened that nothing short of a consciously directed, powerholding organization from the outside would be strong enough to shatter them in order to permit the state hospital to function as a hospital in the truest meaning of the word.

However, since the close of World War II there have been numerous indications that the state hospital as a cultural system will not be permitted much longer to continue along its merry way unimpeded by organized forces from the outside. In fact, World War II proved to be the vehicle for shattering our complacency and lethargy with respect to caring for and treating our mentally ill. The vast number of neuropsychiatric rejectees among the drafted men combined with army psychiatric experience lead quite directly to the passage of the National Mental Health Act. The entrance of the federal government into the mental health field not only gave mental illness a top priority as a public health problem but also mobilized the professional energy for both education and research in this area. This development set the stage for challenging the traditional culture of the state hospital.

The questioning and probing of states about their hospitals by psychiatric leaders, the opening up of state hospitals to social scientists for studying them as social systems, the inaugurating of numerous conferences for dealing with mental health information via radio and television, the allotment of foundation monies for mental health research—all of these events have been additional indications that the century-long isolation of the state mental hospital is at last coming to an end. Now these events can be viewed as initiating forces in the larger community which will make for changes in state hospitals. However, the numerous events pertinent to mental health that are taking place in the larger community and being forged into forces for changing the traditional hospital culture raise a most challenging question for applied social science. The question is this: Should the scientific and professional leaders in the mental health field be content to ride the forces for change in the state mental hospital that are already unlashed in the community, or should they, with all the social-science knowledge that they possess, experiment in developing a new state hospital culture that will provide maximum encouragement and support for the therapeutic process?

Now I realize that this is a big order and may actually be impossible to realize in any complete or final sense, but I am moved to the suggestion for two reasons. First, in England there has already been one attempt to bring such a hospital culture into reality.[5] Secondly—and a pressing concern of social science— the state hospital provides a certain institutional frame, already in existence as a continuing reality, for conducting experiments in the self-conscious building-up of a contrived hospital culture that would maximize therapy. We are stopped, of course, by the fact that we do not know how any hospital culture should function for therapeutic effectiveness but, if our original hypotheses should prove valid, we would have some guide for an experimental production of such a culture.

Whatever we do toward the creating of a new kind of mental-hospital organization, we should proceed experimentally. That is, with the introduction of new plans and devices for dealing with mental patients we should build up some means for measuring their effectiveness. And in so doing we must raise those questions which cut through the traditional practices for dealing with the mentally ill that constitute our past heritage in this area. Should not the size of our state hospitals be reduced drastically? Would it not be desirable to develop for every community a series of 150- or 200-bed hospital clinics, the number dependent on the size of the community, which would serve a local area and be the device for separating those mental patients who can be fitted back into the community from those that cannot? What is the most functional hospital in an architectural sense for treating mental patients? Would it be therapeutically advantageous to develop the mixed-sex ward? What hospital experiences should be provided for the patient which would ease the strain of his return to the community? How should the cost of the system be distributed in the community? Should psychiatric wards be attached to general hospitals as an alternative to the community-hospital clinic? How in the hospital can the available therapeutic resources best be adapted to the problems of the individual patients?

Most of these questions are not new and have been raised by others. I merely repeat them to stimulate further our reflections on the conscious building-up of a new hospital culture. In this area new things are being tried with every passing year, but these new devices lack both a wide acceptance and a knowledge of their validity.

In conclusion, let me mention briefly four relatively new devices which from a logical perspective appear to have some merit and which possibly should be built into our new kind of mental hospital. Here, I am referring to such devices as the work programs geared to the industrial needs of the community found in some mental hospitals in England; the resident hospitals which the patients leave in the morning for their jobs and return in the evening; the orientation courses, workshops and conferences developed for hospital staffs on a continuing basis; and the introduction of the intense socialization program for patients so that every patient is active during the day. These are a few of the new developments which should play a role in any new consciously developed state hospital culture.

By these observations I have attempted to show the character of contemporary state hospital culture and some of the factors pertinent to its development. I have suggested hypothetically that the current state hospital culture will continue to be a liability until in its forms and functioning it will more closely approximate the other institutions in the community. Finally, I have posed the question whether those social forces which are currently acting on the hospital to change it, should not be countered with a more consciously constructed hospital culture which would give us greater assurance of achieving maximum cultural conditions for therapy.

REFERENCES

1. H. W. Dunham and S. K. Weinberg, *The Culture of the State Mental Hospital,* (Detroit, Michigan: Wayne State University Press, 1960) p. 50.
2. "Group Therapy with Chronic Hospitalized Schizophrenia," in E. Brady and F. C. Redlich, eds., *Psychotheraphy with Schizophrenias* (New York: International University Press, 1952), p. 216–230.

3. "A Social Psychological Study of Incontinence," *Psychiatry,* (1950): XIII, 399–416.
4. R. W. Hyde and H. C. Solomon, "Patient Government: A New Form of Group Therapy," *Digest of Neurology and Psychiatry,* 18 (April, 1950): 207–218.
5. See M. Jones, *The Therapeutic Community: A New Treatment Method in Psychiatry* (New York: Basic Books, 1953).

—3—

The Institutional Social Situation: Its Integrating Role in Psychiatric Therapy

Within recent years there have been established in a few countries, notably in England, the Netherlands and the United States what we have called new type psychiatric hospitals and clinics that manifest a rather clear-cut break with the hospitals of the past one hundred years. In this chapter, my central purpose is to portray the significant characteristics of these new type psychiatric institutions along with some of the problems and theoretical issues that are attendant upon their establishment. That is, even in their birth pangs, it is essential to take a closer look at their theoretical foundations in order to prevent, if possible, our present need to do something about psychiatric therapy from undermining our scientific judgement. Consequently, it should be recognized in these remarks that when we refer to these new type institutions we are referring to social structures that are often only in the planning stage or are just getting under way.

Right at the outset we should note that the distinguishing feature of these new institutions is their conscious endeavor to make the institutional social situation a relevant element in therapy. This means that the social situation can be used for organizing and integrating various forms of psychiatric therapy. The social situation, as an aspect of the larger sociocultural environment, has long been recognized as a significant etiological element in some mental illnesses and personality disturbances. It recently has become a relatively important consideration in planning, processing and directing specific therapies for the mental patient.

This increasing recognition of the social situation as a factor in psychiatric therapy is evidenced by the new terms and emphases that have appeared in psychiatric literature during these post-war years. If we listen carefully, we can hear the chorus: "the culture of the mental hospital," "the therapeutic community," "resocialization of the patient," "therapeutic and non-therapeutic staff attitudes," "social therapist," "rehabilitation of the patient," "community psychiatry," "patient self-government," "ward social psychological climates," "lines of communication in the hospital," "socialization of a new doctor," "new nursing roles" and the like. All of these expressions attest to this new emphasis as an attempt to move to some more acceptable level of success in psychiatry.

These theoretical and empirical preoccupations, as indicated by the above expressions, are reflected in the planning and establishment of these new types of clinical and hospital organizations. They differ markedly from those of the past century in at least four respects. These are implicit and often explicit recognitions:

(1) that patients are persons immersed in various kinds of social relationships in the outside world;

(2) that patients with staff personnel constitute a society and culture which can facilitate or hinder the therapeutic process;

(3) that therapy will be more effective when the patient population is kept relatively small;

(4) that the new institutions should be experimental in character. This latter implies that, as the social process of hospital or clinic functions to make the hospital or clinic into an established social structure, a check is imposed by its research orientation which aims to provide new knowledge about the patients, the institution and the therapies.

It is necessary at this point to consider the theory that lies behind these new experiments in psychiatric institutions. While they are in part a reflection of the humanitarianism deeply imbedded in Western culture, they also rest upon certain theoretical considerations about the natures of man and society. Let us begin with society as Cooley viewed it over half a century ago when he stated that the individual and society are twin-born.[1] Society constitutes a web of biological and interactional relationships which act on the individual unit in such a manner that it is gradually fitted into this web in a functional manner. Among humans this web is held together basically through man's capacity to manipulate meaningful symbols or language. Early rudimentary signs evolving gradually into a spoken language represent then the crude beginnings of culture which sets man apart from all other biological forms.

Within this culture which is limited to man, various subcultures emerge which are differentiated particularly by language, but also, by region, class, religion, occupation and specific institutional organizations. It is these latter cultures that have been analyzed in numerous settings by social scientists. Thus, the school, factory, prison, and mental hospital have been studied in order not only to evaluate their influences upon the personality and behavior of persons composing their structures, but also to ascertain some of the unanticipated consequences of their functioning.

But, it is the studies of the mental hospital with which we are concerned. These studies have helped raise to conscious awareness the significance of the ongoing social process within the institution for facilitating or impeding therapy. These studies have further shown that certain unforeseen aspects of this social situation affects patients adversely. They have shown also that the social situation is often a vital part of a specific therapy, and a failure to recognize this, may render the therapy largely ineffective. They have pointed to the culture of the mental hospital as an entity which is often at a marked variance with the culture of other institutions in the same society.[2]

This line of theory and research has been juxtaposed with another line of theory, stemming from depth psychology of which Freud's psychological explorations are basic. Here, the individual originally was viewed as growing and developing within the cauldron of family emotions. Every expression of the biological impulses of the child was repressed, checked and thwarted by the cultural norms as they operated through the parents and other significant persons. In this repression of the impulsive life certain unpleasant experiences tended to be relegated to the unconscious level of the psyche and from there to emerge in the later years as certain physical symptoms or as peculiar and irrational behavior. The very notion of "acting out" behavior, heard often in the clinical setting, implies that the behavior has an irrational quality because it is set in motion by the existence of some, deeply imbedded, unconscious conflict.

This theory, which in its original form was a closed psychological system, however, did view the basic conflicts as arising in social situations previously composed of family members and sometimes other persons connected with the family. Persons whose early traumatic experiences in such situations have lead to twisted adult personalities, also build up, like their more normal fellows, elaborate systems of rationalizations and defenses that are not socially approved and which help to bring about their rejections at the hands of others in the community. Their systems of rationalization and defense function, as in the case of the normals, to keep their peculiarities intact, and with the passage of time they tend to take on an increasing rigid character.

Thus, to the extent that our so-called problem personalities are formed within certain types of social matrices composed of family members and associates, it would seem to follow that if their behavior and personality are to be changed so that they become increasingly acceptable, this must take place in some type of controlled social situation. This controlled social situation must have certain built-in treatment devices which not only bare the original conflict or psychic injury but also break through the unacceptable defenses in order to substitute new and more acceptable ones.

This brings us to the significance of the institutional social situation as a significant element of therapy. Our conscious attempts to create the kind of social situation in our psychiatric institutions to which patients will have responses that are therapeutic is a recognition not only that past social situations have made them into the socially unacceptable personalities that they are, but also that the consciously contrived social situation provides a basis for integrating our various specific therapies into a more meaningful whole. Thus, no matter what therapeutic instrument we use on patients—psychotherapy, group therapy, industrial work, medication, handicraft training or recreational participation—the awareness of the institutional social situation enables patients to have a relationship to one another as part of the total social process. They are, thus, raised to a new level, where, for example, the providing of industrial work is not something that is done to the patient but becomes an instrument which is involved in the social relationship that must perforce take place between the therapist and the patient. This means that it must be meaningful to the patient in terms of his difficulties and that the staff member responsible for it must attempt to see that such meaningfulness is a significant part of the therapeutic social situation.

This integrating role of the social situation is significant in three contexts. First, it involves staff members in a basic way. For, they now must function, not in terms of their traditional roles, but with a keen realization that they, in interaction with the patients, make up the social situation, which they are obligated to make as therapeutic as possible. They, thus, become more than technicians. They are technicians with the added insight that their techniques are part of the social process and go to make up a dynamic social situation. Here, they find themselves responding to patients not only as patients but as persons with personalities and behavior patterns that other persons in the society have defined as being socially unacceptable.

Not only do roles change in these new institutions, but traditional status differentiations between professional groups tend to become blurred. This is likely to happen because in the zeal to create a truly therapeutic climate, there is the attempt to reduce staff tensions and conflicts because of their often unfavorable impact on the patient. Staff members gradually became aware that, if a therapeutic climate is to emerge, there will be a necessity to discuss problems and issues involving staff and patients in a more complete fashion. Thus, the authority and prestige of a status position is less likely to operate in arriving at a decision, but the decision will be permitted to emerge on the basis of available facts and a discussed interpretation of them. This, as I have indicated, brings about a blurring of status positions within the institution.

The third context has to do with what constitutes a cure for these patients. For, if our theory is correct, patients have become patients, because of certain experiences tied to reoccurring social situations which have forced them further and further away from the approved patterns of conduct. Thus, a cure constitutes no specific state of personality integration but rather a resocialization or a newly acquired capacity to fit into some societal niche in such a way that the patient ceases to be a problem to those others who form his milieu and the larger community. This implies that within a given social system there may be as many different kinds of cures as there are subcultures. It has been said that the mark of the civilized man is the capacity to manage his frustrations. And so with our patients, we have helped them along the path of cure when we have succeeded in bringing them to a point where they can manage their impulses and frustrations with psychic defenses that are socially acceptable. This conception of a "cure" in the frame of our theory makes it necessary for the therapist to be aware of the possibilities of milieu therapy in lieu of an exclusive concern to reduce or eliminate the ravages of intra-psychic conflict.

Perhaps, this will be sufficient for providing some conception about my views concerning the nature and significance of the institutional social situation. I now wish to turn to some of the problems and theoretical issues which confront us as we strive to mold the psychiatric institution into a consciously contrived social situation and to conceptualize its role in the therapeutic process.

Let me make it clear that in discussing certain troublesome problems that confront us in the new kinds of psychiatric institutions, I am doing it within a decided policy of initiating them. This means that we are constantly on the search for more effective methods to create the type of social institution that will be most therapeutic for various types of patients.

What are these troublesome problems? First and foremost, it seems to me, the question must be raised as to the type of patients that should be selected for these new institutions. Do we have any valid criteria that can govern our selection of patients? Should we select certain patients that in a given diagnostic judgment are most likely to be helped? Or should our selection be a random one from our universe of available patients? Or should we select one half whose prognosis is good balanced with a half whose prognosis is poor? Should we attempt to eliminate at the outset those patients whose illnesses are basically organic in character? Or should we include some of these latter in the new settings? Perhaps, there is some way of determining those patients who will be most responsive to these new social climates. Here, at the outset, it would seem we must clarify our ideas about our objectives both with respect to therapy and research before we can decide upon the most desirable selection pattern.

Secondly, it would seem that we must have some rather concrete notion of what a therapeutic culture is like. Should we attempt to contrive an institutional culture that is of similar quality to that of other institutions in the society? Or should we attempt to contrive an institutional culture that expresses some more idealized version? My choice here would be the first alternative because any other version of institutional culture would constitute a social climate that would not prepare patients for the rigors and vicissitudes of the free community. While the answer in terms of our therapeutic goal seems clear here, I do think that in initiating these new kinds of institutions, we should bring this problem to the forefront of our discussion.

Thirdly, how can we build up a morale and consensus which will make the institutional culture of definite therapeutic value and at the same time preserve a flexibility in dealing individually with certain patients without doing damage to the cultural forms of the entire unit? In a certain sense this is the same problem which many of our contemporary societies are facing when they attempt to bring about a balance of forces that will preserve a maximum of personal freedom for individuals and at the same time maintain a security for everybody.

As corollary here, the conscious contriving of an institutional culture implies that many of the traditional activity therapies must be re-examined in order to find the pattern of procedure that will be most therapeutically effective. An example of this might be Maxwell Jones' account[3] of how mixing the sexes in an industrial work shop made for a closer tie with the outside reality situation for the patients and hence brought about more adequate therapeutic responses.

Fourthly, the professional personnel at all levels in these new type institutions face a problem of observation. They must learn to distinguish between behavior of patients that is a response to situations growing out of various kinds of interactions—patient-patient, staff-staff, or staff-patient—and that behavior which is of an acting out type and flows from their unconscious conflicts and so is unrelated to the evolving social situation. However, such behavior may sometimes impinge on the social situation and even affect it in diverse ways. This is the distinction which Caudill in his study of a psychiatric ward[4] so cogently analyzed when he showed that the psychoanalysts in dealing with individual patients refused to give credence to the existence of a ward social situation but merely dealt with all patients' verbalizations of it as symptomatic of their underlying emotional conflicts.

The capacity to make this distinction depends on

training essential for the professional personnel that is to work in these new psychiatric settings. For unless one can come to conceptualize this distinction, one will not only make mistakes in dealing with patients but also will not be aware of the evolving hospital culture with the ever present necessity to mold it in a direction conducive to therapy.

Let us turn to one final problem of role changes to which we already referred as distinctive of these new institutions. This problem arises from the fact that all staff members, professional or otherwise, are frequently thrust into new roles and ones which were not envisioned in their training. This is because the new institutional milieu has an awareness with respect to its purpose and hence is likely to be quite unorthodox, while the professional training of staff members is mostly likely to have been of a traditional orthodox variety. Consequently, staff members will experience certain tensions and anxieties during their adjustments to their new but unorthodox professional roles. This is an inevitable concomitant of this type of institution because in it the traditional staff-patient relationship undergoes a marked change as both patient and staff member attempt to get a view of themselves within a dynamic social system. Such a social system is expected to have therapeutic consequences for the patient, but it is also likely to be unsettling to the staff member until he grasps the connection between his role and the other roles in creating the institutional culture.

I wish now to turn to some of the theoretical issues which the development of these new institutions inevitably poses. Here, I am speaking from a position outside of them and attempting to examine some issues that are bound to have a bearing on the consideration of policy aiming to establish them.

First, there is the question as to whether or not these new type of institutions should be considered primarily as research opportunities for analyzing patients as well as for integrating therapeutic techniques. If priority is given to research rather than therapy, how will it be possible to orient all staff members to the view that research is the primary purpose and that therapy is merely an incidental by-product? Here, those professionals that are trained primarily for service present a real obstacle. It is very difficult to fit them into a purely research situation. On the other hand, it is possible to combine both research and therapy in the same institutional set-up. In this latter instance, will it be possible to mold the professionals into a team that has a sound grasp of both goals? This is very necessary if conflict is to be avoided between those professionals who are primarily research-minded and those who are concerned solely with therapy.

If, on the other hand, we have primarily a therapeutic concern in the development of these new type institutions, will it be feasible to incorporate within them some research design that is directed to a continual evaluation of what is achieved by the new institution? Because it seems to me that in a final sense we want to have a clearcut picture of the patients with whom therapy was successful and why as well as the opposite picture of patients with whom therapy was a failure and why. For if the new institutions are to be continued and additional ones inaugurated, we must have a sound basis for asserting their superiority over the traditional types of institutions.

A second issue which also has many facets to it arises when we raise the question of fitting the "cured" patient into the free community. For, if these new institutions are successful this means that there will be proportionally more cures to be fitted into the community. We face further the problem of determining if a cure achieved in the institutions and certified by the professional staff will at the same time be recognized as a cure in the community milieu to which the recovered patients must return. Here, it may be relevant to note that the underlying theory behind the new institutions points to the possibility that there may be almost as many type cures as there are subcultures within a given social system. This observation only reinforces our previous remark that the final test of a cure is a capacity of the patient to find a niche in a community where he functions in such a fashion that his behavior is supported and reinforced by others in his milieu. But, there is also one other very realistic aspect of cures that should be taken into account. We want to be able to show by quantitative measurement that our new type institutions can show a recovery rate that is significantly higher than pure chance—that is the percentage of those who "recover" if nothing at all is done for them —or that among those who do "recover" the duration of illness has been considerably shortened.

A third theoretical issue emerges when we face the question as to how far we can carry our therapeutic efforts with the mentally ill and disturbed personalities that come to official attention in human society. For, if we operate from the theoretical position that certain forms of these numerous abnormalities are sociologically induced—and many of our therapeutic techniques in the new institutions proceed from this assumption—then our therapeutic efforts will continue with a selected number of these personalities while, at the same time, our social system will continue to grind out year after year practically the same number of these type mental cases providing that the same societal conditions continue to prevail.

On the other hand, if our science eventually establishes a biological or physiological etiology for these mental disturbances then we may be able to develop new therapeutic and even preventive techniques which may eliminate, or at least considerably reduce, these illnesses from human society as has been the case with other diseases. However, if our first assumption is valid, then we face a situation with these types of personalities which is comparable to the crime phenomenon in some countries, that is, the yearly number of sociological mental cases like the number of criminals will continue to remain relatively constant under the same social conditions. This means that our therapy as in the case of criminals will be eventually directed towards keeping these twisted personalities out of the hospital and, if they get in, to direct our therapeutic techniques, as we do now, to provide them with sufficiently integrated and acceptable self-conceptions that will enable them to fit into and find a place for themselves in the free community. The chief problem that arises at this point is the extent of the capacity of a given society to absorb back these personalities that have been straightened out by therapy. I do not know the answer here, but I would predict that as a given society becomes more bureaucratized and homogeneous, this task will become more difficult. This may also have its brighter side because such a society may produce a decreasing number of these abnormal mental and personality types.

Finally, there is the related issue of the distribution of costs. Therapy of a psychological and sociological variety is, like education, an expensive proposition. How can we weight the cost of therapy as over against costs directed at prevention? In some way we must try to assess the costs of therapy as over against the costs required to strengthen our existing social institutions—the school, the family, the industry and the preventive health agency. If the society produces a limited number of psychiatrists should we use more of them at the level of the school or in the hospital, after the damage has been done? Or should more of them be asked to concentrate on research rather than on therapy? I am not sure that we have any good answers to these questions, but I raise this problem because I think that we should have a keen awareness of this perplexing issue as we plan various research, preventive and therapeutic programs which always take place within a framework of limited resources.

In discussing what I have called problems and theoretical issues involved in the operation and planning of these psychiatric institutions, I wish to make it clear that I have done nothing more than scratch the surface. But I think what I have discussed are matters highly pertinent to these new therapeutic endeavours. In these remarks I have focused on four things.

First, I have tried, even though too briefly, to show the converging lines of social and psychological theory with some supporting empirical work that has led to the inauguration of these newer kinds of psychiatric institutions.

Secondly, I have tried to point to those features of the new institutions which distinguish them from the traditional ones.

Thirdly, I went on to pose some problems that confront us immediately in these new institutions within an agreed upon policy for inaugurating them.

Finally, I attempted to explore some of the theoretical issues which can hardly be avoided as we endeavor both to add to our knowledge of patients and to increase our therapeutic successes. These are the issues which should come up before policy is decided.

It is too soon to assess results, but, it seems to me, that our big concern should be to try and keep these new institutions dynamic, experimental, and tentative and to prevent them from being absorbed in the bureaucratic structure of modern society. For, if this latter eventually comes about we will find ourselves in an intolerable mess where we shall probably never learn what has happened and how successful or unsuccessful we have been. However, all we can do in respect to this problem as is the case with any problem is to take the most appropriate actions on the basis of the meagre knowledge that we possess. For the stern day to day realities of the social process wait for no man and least of all do they wait until we perfect our knowledge about them. Perhaps, Santayana's lines in one of his sonnets best expresses our sense of inadequacy in the face of reality.

> Our knowledge is but a torch of smoky pine,
> Which lights our pathway just one step ahead
> Across a void of mystery and dread.

REFERENCES

1. C. H. Cooley, Human Nature and the Social Order (New York: Charles Scribner & Sons, 1902), p. 51.
2. J. F. Bateman and H. W. Dunham, "The State Mental Hospital as a Specialized Community Experience," *American Journal of Psychiatry,* 103 (1948): 621–633; H. Rowland, "Interactional Processes in the State Mental Hospital," *Psychiatry,* 1 (1938): 323–332; A. Stanton and M. Schwartz, The Mental Hospital: A Study of Institutional Participation in Psychiatric Illness and Treatment (New York: Basic Books, 1953).
3. M. Jones, B. A. Pomryn and E. Skellern, "Work Therapy," *Lancet,* 270 (1956): 343–344.

4. W. Caudill, F. Redlich, H. Gilmore and E. Brady, "Social Structure and Interactional Processes on a Psychiatric Ward," *American Journal of Orthopsychiatry,* 22 (1952): 314–344.

—4—

Community Mental Health Centers: Therapeutic and Sociological Problems of Transition

In this chapter I focus upon some of the therapeutic and sociological problems that are emerging as we move toward the development of community mental health centers in the various countries of the Western world. Community mental health has many of the characteristics of a social movement embodying, as it does, a new idea in the treatment of the mentally ill, some enthusiastic proponents among psychiatrists of several countries and a host of energetic supporters in the auxiliary psychiatric professions and in numerous lay groups. It is, perhaps, a sign of the speediness of communication today when

Read before Sixth International Congress of Psychotherapy, August 27, 1964, London.

there appear to be so many simultaneous stirrings in various countries of the Western world with respect to community mental health. Bremer[1] has reported from Norway, Stromgren[2] has outlined its developments in Denmark, Lawson[3] writes about the Saskatchewan plan in Canada, Freeman[4] discusses the situation in Great Britain, Strotzka[5] analyzes the situation in central Europe, as well as several investigators reporting from the United States,[6] all focusing their remarks on various aspects of community mental health centers as they are taking shape.

Before attempting to come to grips with some of the problems in the transition to community mental health centers that constitute my focus of attention here, I must confront two tasks. First, I want to describe as compactly as possible what appears to be emerging as representing the central characteristics of community mental health programs, and second, I want to take account of some of the factors that have served to push psychiatric treatment in this direction.

Community mental health programs all appear to have one central idea. This idea appears to embody the principle of unifying and integrating diagnosis, treatment, rehabilitation and prevention facilities as they have often developed in isolation from one another in the various communities. Since the war many new facilities concerned with the treatment of the mentally ill have developed, such as night hospitals, day hospitals, industrial units attached to state hospitals, psychiatric wards of general hospitals, various specialized outpatient clinics—al-

coholism, drug addiction, geriatrics, emotional problems of children, various rehabilitation services,
halfway houses for adolescents, and the like. Many of
these new facilities have developed in connection
with the traditional state hospitals and many of them
have developed in isolation from one another under
both private and public auspices. This situation has
produced in many countries, and especially in the
United States, a veritable network of psychiatric
agencies which makes the problem of determining
the size and character of the mental health problem
a most difficult and precarious undertaking. The
community mental health movement envisions the
unifying and integrating of these new treatment and
rehabilitative facilities at some central point in the
community in order to provide total psychiatric service and thus insure continuity of care for a delimited
population. A community mental health center
model that is often portrayed pictures a small psychiatric hospital of 150 to 300 beds with an evaluating
service, an attached day hospital, a night hospital, an
outpatient clinic, a community aid program, and a
home psychiatric service which would serve a community of from 150,000 to 300,000 people. It is, of
course, well recognized that this model will vary,
depending upon the cultural and demographic characteristics of the population that is to be served.

Some idea as to what is envisioned by the community mental health movement can be had by a
careful comparison of Figures 4.1 and 4.2. In Figure
4.1 is portrayed the contemporary organization of

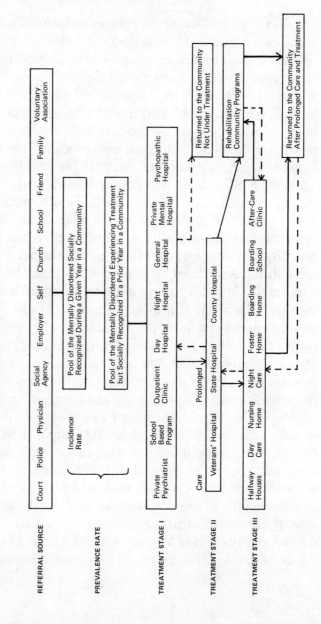

Figure 4.1. IDEAL STRUCTURE OF CURRENT ORGANIZATION OF PSYCHIATRIC FACILITIES IN THE COMMUNITIES AND STATES IN THE UNITED STATES

REFERRAL SOURCE

Court · Police · Physician · Social Agency · Employer · Self · Church · School · Friend · Family · Voluntary Association

PREVALENCE RATE

Incidence Rate

Pool of the Mentally Disordered Socially Recognized During a Given Year in a Community

Pool of the Mentally Disordered Experiencing Treatment but Socially Recognized in a Prior Year in a Community

TREATMENT STAGE I

Private Psychiatrist · School Based Program · Outpatient Clinic · Day Hospital · Night Hospital · General Hospital · Private Mental Hospital · Psychopathic Hospital

TREATMENT STAGE II

Care · Prolonged

Veterans' Hospital · State Hospital · County Hospital

TREATMENT STAGE III

Halfway Houses · Day Care · Nursing Home · Night Care · Foster Home · Boarding Home · Boarding School · After-Care Clinic

Returned to the Community Not Under Treatment

Rehabilitation Community Programs

Returned to the Community After Prolonged Care and Treatment psychiatric facilities along with the referral sources as they currently exist in the various communities of the United States. It is well recognized, of course, that the majority of communities do not have such a complete network of psychiatric facilities. For the most part communities are serviced by a state hospital with an outpatient clinic attached and with a child guidance center completely separated from the state hospital. In Figure 4.2 there is portrayed an ideal organization of psychiatric facilities as they would be related in a community mental health center. Such centers would include all preventive, treatment, rehabilitative and research functions essential for a complete psychiatric program and would have a central location within the community.

In Chapter 2, I attempted to analyze the issue as to whether the creation of the so-called therapeutic milieu could have real therapeutic significance for the patients. There I expressed skepticism as to whether such milieus would really have a therapeutic value for patients but I was most enthusiastic about the need to develop such milieus in order to break the cultural cake of the traditional state hospital toward the end of heightening the interest, emotional involvement and morale of persons who are concerned with studying, treating and caring for the mentally ill. In Chapter 3, I dealt with the role of the institutional social situation for serving as an integrating focus to the various psychiatric therapies within the hospital and saw again this development as taking place largely in the state hospitals of several Western countries. At the time of writing, I did not

Figure 4.2.   IDEAL STRUCTURE OF PROPOSED COMMUNITY MENTAL HEALTH CENTERS IN THE UNITED STATES

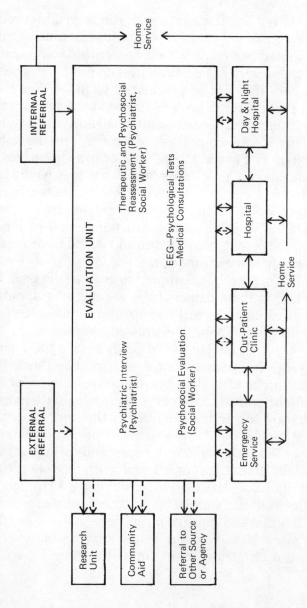

*Adapted from *A Comprehensive Psychiatric Center: Concept and Structure* by Fritz A. Freyhan and Julia A. Mayo, U.S. Department of Health, Education & Welfare.

visualize the significance of the community mental health movement, the rumblings of which were just beginning to be heard. Rather, I saw these attempts as something which would try to increase the therapeutic potential of the traditional state hospital.

But, as I have tried to show in the charts, the community mental health center makes a clear break with the past and in fact has as one of its central concerns the attempt to break down the age-old isolation between the mental hospital and the community and to provide an opportunity for the various professionals who work in the mental hospital to become reorganized and reintegrated relative to the community.

The various types of experience that have served to create the community mental health movement have been both numerous and effective. Certain attitudes that are sounded constantly in the literature, such as the belief that many psychiatrists hold that psychiatric facilities should be as available in the treatment of mental illness as are current facilities for the treatment of physical illness plus the stated attitude that people, now at this time, consider that they have a right to a reasonable adjustment,[7] have served as rationalistic cornerstones of the movement. But behind these attitudes there is a variety of experiences that have provided a more optimistic outlook with respect to mental illness than have previously been present. Whether or not this optimistic outlook will be justified only time will tell, for we will not be able to ascertain the results of maximizing our treatment potential through the inauguration of the community mental health centers until we have had a decade or two of experience with them.

The gradual recognition following World War II in the United States and Western European countries that mental illness was a number one public health problem, has served as a spur to action. The experience with ataractic drugs showing that many mental patients, including schizophrenics, could be maintained in the community, has certainly been one of the factors contributing to a more optimistic outlook with respect to mental illness. Even here, however, the problem of the illness was not solved, but the locus of care tended to shift from the hospital to the community. Again, the growth of private psychiatric practice, particularly in the United States, following World War II, provided psychiatrists with a wealth of experience concerning those persons in the population that needed some sort of psychiatric help. These patients, of course, were not the same type that one found in the old state mental hospitals, but rather represented people with problems showing many of the symptoms that seemed to characterize the old hard-core cases. This kind of experience helped to widen the conception as to the role that psychiatry should play in the treatment of persons in various stages of maladjustment, and as such, added to the optimism with respect to the efficacy of treatment.

Another factor that has represented an additional push toward the community mental health idea is reflected by the various sociological studies of the mental hospital.[8] These studies have subjected the mental hospital to a careful, clinical appraisal toward the end of evaluating its effectiveness as a therapeutic agent for the mentally ill. The analysis of the inherent conflict between protection for the community and therapeutic treatment, the portrayal of the often-covert opposition between the attendant staff and the patient group, the laying bare of the mental hospital as a distinct institutional culture which incorporated the professionals within it thus serving to block its therapeutic goal, the portrayal of the manner in which staff conflicts engender disturbances in certain patients, and finally, the delineation of the differences between the values sought by the patients and those sought by the staff, are some of the findings that have served to hold the mental hospital up as an ineffective therapeutic instrument. Thus, these studies have served to light up the traditional dissatisfactions concerning the mental hospital that have been present for some time among those professionals who have seen the wisdom in Florence Nightengale's statement: "Whatever else hospitals do, they should not spread disease." These studies also, by their total impact, have tended to question whether the best results and the lowest social and economic costs are secured by the large state hospitals which have housed in the United States from 2,000 to 10,000 patients.

One final factor that has played a role in bringing about this ferment for community mental health centers has been the increased communication and contact between European and American psychiatric professionals following World War II. This has resulted in a literal crystallization of ideas when

Americans viewed firsthand some of the plans and programs that were brought forward in the European countries, and the Europeans have had the opportunity to assess American psychiatric experience.

As plans go forward in the various countries of the Western world to bring into reality the promises of the community mental health movement which are aimed at maximizing the treatment potential that may already exist in a given community, it is necessary to take stock of some of the emergent therapeutic and sociological problems that are bound to follow in the wake of this transition. It is hoped that a developing awareness and a consideration of such problems will serve to smooth the transition to the new organization of treatment facilities.

Let us consider three of these problems which border upon therapeutic concerns and which, when answered in a certain way, tend to shape the character of the new psychiatric centers. First, let us consider the issue of therapeutic priority. It is expected that these new centers will have treatment facilities for dealing with all types of psychiatric problems, and ideally, it is expected that each person served by such a facility will probably obtain the maximum benefit that is possible for his particular mental disturbance. However, the center will have, it is assumed, a psychiatric service, an outpatient clinic for the treating of the mild neurotic and character disturbances that can continue to live in the community, a day and night hospital for rehabilitative efforts after psychiatric treatment to ease the transition of the patient back into the community and a home service for emergency and later rehabilitative treatment in the home. The question arises whether such a center will develop priorities of emphasis in the treatment services that it offers. To what extent will the staff tend to direct its energies more and more to the mildly disturbed patients and the emergency treatment cases and continue to neglect the hardcore psychotics because they are less likely to respond to the treatment devices that are available? Now such an emphasis might easily be predicted because one can hardly blame professional therapists for wanting to work with those patients that are responsive to therapy. On the other hand, over the long run, the continuation of such an emphasis would mean a neglect of the possibility of raising researchable questions with respect to the hard-core psychotic and thus would serve as a barrier to the advancement of knowledge about this group.

A second therapeutic problem arises with respect to a shift in emphasis that is often visualized in the planning for these new community mental health centers. This new perspective points to the preventive role that such centers should play. Here, prevention means the development of effective treatment methods at the collective level to supplement clinical approaches. This has frequently meant that certain psychiatrists of the community mental health center would serve as consultants to groups, institutions and other organizations in the community toward the end of improving interpersonal relationships within them and directing their practices and activities along lines that would be supposedly conducive to mental health. Now, this is a big order, and perhaps we would never be able to determine whether such activities would actually in the long run reduce the incidence of emotional disturbances in the community. There is a certain amount of evidence in connection with the hard-core psychoses, particularly schizophrenia, that such effort would be largely in vain. Whether it might play a role in the reduction of certain minor emotional disturbances such as neuroses and character disorders, of course, remains to be seen. However, it is difficult to conceive that such consultation would actually have any effect on the incidence of these disturbances in the community as the character of family and the institutional dynamics is so tied up with the historical and prevailing cultural factors that the production of these milder disorders would continue barring a total and complete reorganization of social institutions within another value system. Even here, such a reorganization might only mean that the old forms of the minor disturbances would disappear but completely new forms would arise. In other words, a high probability of the success of prevention is extremely uncertain and while we all like to give lip service to the idea of prevention we are not likely to be successful in any preventive efforts until we have a clearer conception of the etiological factors that lie behind the several disorders. It is possible that in those mental disorders which have more of a genetic and biophysiological base that we can develop, eventually, devices for both treatment and prevention. However, if eventually it is established that certain mental and emotional disorders are a developmental phenomenon, exacerbated by certain noxious factors in the environment, then it is doubtful if these disturbances will yield to preventive efforts barring a reconstruction of human nature and a restructuring and strengthening of the societal institutions. This is a most complex problem. Within the entire framework of a preventive policy there are significant considerations of social values which are extremely difficult to confront and to resolve. The issue of freedom for the human personality, and, at the same time, placing checks on the human personality in order to achieve a stable collective life, is an age-old problem of the Western world and it is doubtful whether it ever will be resolved. These two necessities of our common existence are always in a precarious balance.

Finally, there has been a mounting search since World War II for alternatives to the hospitalization of mental patients. The development of the new pharmaceuticals has speeded and abetted this search. The emphasis on rehabilitation of mental patients has also played a role here. The experiences of Querido in Amsterdam[9] have served to point to the possibility of treatment in the community for many mental patients as a substitute for hospitalization. Now these developments have probably helped to shift the locus for certain mental patients from the hospital to the community with the resulting possibility of an increase in home visiting by psychiatrists and the development of various rehabilitative activity to keep the patient busy in the community. It has also resulted in the continuing search for certain kinds of social niches into which selected mental patients who show some level of recovery, even though not complete, can be fitted, where they will constitute only minimum problems to themselves and others. This shift of locus for certain mental patients points to one developing direction that the new community mental health centers may take.[10]

However, perhaps the sociological problems which the new community mental health center will face are even more pressing and acute. There is, of course, the problem of defining the limits of the community and the size of the population that is to be served. This means that some careful analysis must be made of the age, sex and ethnic structure of a given population in order to estimate the number and types of patients that will be thrown off from such a population. This implies also that the community mental health center will have to adapt its organization and services to the character of the population that is to be served. This problem, of course, may become more acute in large urban areas where ideally a number of such community health centers would have to be developed, again dependent upon the size and character of the population. The problem becomes still more acute, particularly in the United States, because of the instability experienced by so many urban communities resulting from a large turnover in population, which means that many families in the course of a year would be shifting their locus from the area served by one center to the area served by another center. This immediately raises problems of their relationship with staff members in whom they have confidence that whets their desire to return to the old center. However, there is little doubt that the community mental health center in the urban area will face problems that are of a completely different character than the community mental health center in a more stable rural community.

Second, with the development of these new community mental health centers which largely will be publicly supported in much the same way as the old state hospitals are publicly supported, there will be repeated a conflict between the policies of centralization versus decentralization with respect to their control. The trend, certainly in the United States, seems to be in the direction of centralization, supposedly in the interest of cost, but with centralization there goes the development of increased bureaucratic red tape which serves to take the professionals away from the therapeutic and research problems presented by the mental patient.

Third, there is the problem of achieving an integration between the new community mental health centers and the already existing public health and public welfare facilities. This is no easy task because existing organizations already have a certain traditional pride in their accomplishments, and they are likely to resent an integration if it should in any way interfere with their power and authority. Admittedly, these problems are difficult, but can be resolved with a clear recognition that our common task is to maximize treatment and prevention potentialities for the mentally ill in any community.

Fourth, the system of community mental health centers, like the plan for the reorganization of state hospitals in terms of serving a certain geographical unit,[11] calls for a big shift in professional roles. It means that departments of psychiatry, psychology, social work, nursing and occupational therapy are likely to be broken up in the attempt to focus the skills of these professionals upon the patient and his needs. It further implies that the professionals build either a democratic teamwork of equality or a more authoritative structure which is likely to be under the dominance of the most qualified and highly trained professional, which in most instances would probably be the psychiatrist. This, of course, implies that professional identification would be weakened, but would still continue to exist and might in fact be strengthened in the separate professional organizations in the community. Such a development would tend to minimize departmental friction which has always continued to exist in the old type hospital organization.

Finally, there is a problem that centers in the relationship between a valid view of American society and the image of American society frequently portrayed in the "educational materials" of the community mental health movement. As one reads some of the more propagandistic literature concerning the creation of community mental health centers, it appears that the writers have in mind an American community which is perhaps a part of the American dream but which is simply not true. This image seems to consist, with its shifting perspective due to variations in income, of rows of neat little houses, each surrounded by a picket fence with geraniums on the window sills, with carefully tended lawns, well preserved and well cared for, stretching out away from the collection of stores which services the people in the community and with schools and churches scattered throughout the area. It is a community where people are friendly, where they support their local institutions, where they raise and care for their children, and where life goes on within a fixed rhythm year after year and generation after generation. In short, it is the kind of conception that Thornton Wilder portrays in *Our Town*. It is a picture of our community life that we sometimes peddle abroad and which is evident in our movies and television programs. These mythical communities, of course, have various problems but their citizens would always deal with them in an orderly, sensible, rational and humane fashion with varying degrees of success. Sometimes it seems to me that we have come to a point where many of us have become victims of our own propaganda. What I am describing is a community life that, with some minor exceptions in isolated, rural areas, does not exist in contemporary America. For America, since 1900, has become a nation of cities and the people in these cities appear to be constantly on the move. In fact, (as of 1964) 4,000,000 persons, which constitutes approximately 2.2 percent of the population, are currently living in mobile homes. In addition, there is a constant in- and out-migration that characterizes our cities to the extent that in certain communities of our large metropolitan areas three quarters of the population will have turned over within the space of five years. In these metropolitan areas, it is approximated that 20 percent will have changed their residence during any one year—some staying within the same area and others moving to new metropolitan areas. These two factors of urbanization and mobility which I have cited are realities which change population structures in our communities and result in their lack of stability.

Now, this picture is relevant to our vision of the new community mental health centers because far from serving a population which comes from an ideal community setting where neighbors know each other, these community centers will be set down for the most part in urban areas where they will constantly be serving a changing population. The health records that are to be kept must follow the patient when he moves. This, in turn, does not mean that community mental health centers should not be developed, but only that we should be cognizant of the changing character of the population they will be asked to serve and so adapt them accordingly. They will no more serve a stable community of people than our respective urban draft boards represent the neighbors of those boys who are to be drafted into the American army.

In this paper I started with an analysis of the social forces that have shaped the contours of community mental health viewed as a social movement.

I then attempted to present the organizational structure of the old systems as contrasted with the ideal structure of the community mental health centers that are in the process of development. In the transition I have attempted to point to certain specific therapeutic and sociological problems that will definitely condition their development and the functioning of the therapeutic program. It is hoped that an anticipation of these problems will facilitate a smoother development of community mental health centers aimed at the maximization of treatment potential for the mentally ill throughout the world.

REFERENCES

1. Johan Bremer, "Community Mental Health in Norway," *Proceedings of the Third World Congress of Psychiatry,* 3, (Montreal, Canada: McGill University and University of Toronto Presses, 1961): 72–75.
1. Erik Stromgren, "The Psychiatric Hospital as Centre of Community Psychiatry," *Comprehensive Psychiatry,* 4 (6) (December, 1963): 433–441.
3. F. S. Lawson, "The Saskatchewan Plan," *Proceedings of the Third World Congress of Psychiatry,* 3 (Montreal, Canada: McGill University and University of Toronto Presses, 1961): 62–64.
4. Hugh Freeman, "Community Mental Health Action in Great Britain," *Proceedings of the Third World Congress of Psychiatry,* 1 (Montreal, Can-

ada: McGill University and University of Toronto Presses, 1961): 292–295.

5. Hans Strotzka, "Community Mental Health in Central Europe and With Refugees," *Proceedings of the Third World Congress of Psychiatry,* 3 (Montreal, Canada: McGill University and University of Toronto Presses, 1961): 64–67.

6. See Viola W. Bernard, "Some Interrelationships of Training for Community Psychiatry, Community Mental Health Programmes, and Research in Social Psychiatry," *Proceedings of the Third World Congress of Psychiatry,* 3 (Montreal, Canada: McGill University and University of Toronto Presses, 1961): 67–71; Bertram Brown, "Home Visiting by Psychiatrists," *Proceedings of the Third World Congress of Psychiatry,* 1 (Montreal, Canada: McGill University and University of Toronto Presses, 1961): 241–245; Herbert Dorken, "Behind the Scenes in Community Mental Health," *American Journal of Psychiatry,* 119 (4) (October, 1962): 328–335; Julia A. Mayo, "Community Psychiatry: A Challenge for Social Work," *Comprehensive Psychiatry,* 4 (6) (December, 1963): 409–416.

7. Herbert Dorken, "Behind The Scenes in Community Mental Health," *American Journal of Psychiatry,* 119 (4) (October, 1962): 328–335.

8. Ivan Belknap, *Human Problems of a State Mental Hospital* (New York: McGraw-Hill, 1956); William Caudill, *The Psychiatric Hospital as A Small Society* (Cambridge, Massachusetts: Harvard University Press for Commonwealth Fund,

1958); H. Warren Dunham and S. Kirson Weinberg, *The Culture of the State Mental Hospital* (Detroit: Wayne State University Press, 1960); Renee C. Fox, *Experiment Perilous: Physicians and Patients Facing the Unknown* (Glencoe, Ill.: The Free Press, 1959); A. Stanton and M. Schwartz, *The Mental Hospital: A Study of Institutional Participation in Psychiatric Illness and Treatment* (New York: Basic Books, 1954); R. Williams, M. Greenblat, and P. Levinson, eds., *The Patient and the Mental Hospital* (Glencoe, Ill.: The Free Press, 1957).

9. A. Querido, "Early Diagnosis and Treatment Services," *The Elements of a Community Mental Health Program* (New York: Milbank Memorial Fund, 1955), pp. 1–24.

10. H. E. Freeman and O. G. Simmons, "The Social Integration of Former Mental Patients," *International Journal of Social Psychiatry*, 4 (4) (Spring, 1959), 264–271.

11. C. L. Bennett, "The Dutchess County Project for Community Mental Health," *Proceedings of the Third World Congress of Psychiatry*, 3 (Montreal, Canada: McGill University and University of Toronto Presses, 1961): 75–78.

—5—

Community Psychiatry: The Newest Therapeutic Bandwagon

The proposal to add community psychiatry to the ever-widening list of psychiatric specialties deserves a critical examination. Thus, my purpose in this chapter is fourfold. First, I intend to examine the nature of community psychiatry as it is taking shape. Second, I want to consider our continuing uncertainty about mental illness which is manifested in a widening of its definition. Third, I will discuss some of the historical landmarks and cultural forces that have brought about the proposal for this new subspecialty of psychiatry. Finally, I will examine some of its

Read before the staff of the Institute for Juvenile Research, Chicago, Illinois, May 19, 1964. Reprinted from *Archives of General Psychiatry,* XII (March 1965), 303–313. Copyright 1965 by American Medical Association.

hidden aspects with respect to the future role of psychiatry.

COMMUNITY PSYCHIATRY: THE NEWEST SUBSPECIALTY

Let us begin by examining the nature of community psychiatry that is apparently emerging, as judged by a mounting chorus of voices from those who jump on any moving bandwagon. In doing this, I will focus first on community psychiatry in relation to community mental health and the various programs, plans, and social actions that are currently getting under way, with emphases that are as varied as the cultural-regional contrasts of American society.

A pattern concerned with maximizing treatment potential for the mentally ill is gradually taking shape. This newest emphasis points to a declining role of the traditional state hospital and the rise of the community mental health center with all of the attendant essential auxiliary services for the treatment of the mentally ill. In its ideal form, the community mental health center would provide psychiatric services, both diagnostic and treatment, for all age groups, and for both inpatients and outpatients in a particular community. In addition, day and night hospitals, convalescent homes, and rehabilitative programs would be closely connected to the center, as well as any other service that helps toward the maximizing of treatment potential with respect to the characteristics of the population that it is designed to serve. Also attached to this center would be several kinds of research activities aimed at evaluating and experimenting with old and new therapeutic procedures. The state hospital would, in all likelihood, remain in the background, for those patients who seemingly defy all efforts with available therapeutic techniques to fit them back into family and community with an assurance of safety to themselves and others. This reorganization of psychiatric facilities as a community mental health program would also imply an increased and workable co-ordination of diverse social agencies in the community to detect and refer those persons who need psychiatric help.

This ideal structure does appear to be oriented toward the urban community. Therefore, the need arises to clarify the size and type of the population that would be served. Further, a breakdown of the population into age and sex categories along with several projected estimates of the number of mentally ill persons who will be found in these population categories would be required. Estimates should be made for the psychoneuroses, the psychoses, the psychopathies, the mentally retarded, and the geriatric cases that will be found in a community.

Indeed, we should attempt to mobilize and organize our psychiatric resources in order to maximize existing therapeutic potential for any community. At all events, certain professionals at the National Institute of Mental Health believe that if a realistic community mental health program comes into existence, there must be a community psychiatry that knows how to use it. While the logic here escapes me, it seems to be quite clear to Viola Bernard, who states: "Recognition of the need to augment the conventional training for mental health personnel to equip them for the newer function of community mental health practice parallels wide-scale trends toward more effective treatment methods at the collective level to augment one-to-one clinical approaches."[1] Dr. Bernard goes on to say that community psychiatry can be regarded as a subspecialty of psychiatry and that it embraces three major subdivisions —social psychiatry, administrative psychiatry, and public health psychiatry.

While Dr. Bernard may clearly see the nature of a community psychiatry that transcends the traditional one-to-one clinical approach, this is not the case with departments of psychiatry in some medical schools, as the recent National Institute of Mental Health survey attests.[2] In reviewing the limited literature, it is all too clear that different conceptions abound as to what community psychiatry is. While these conceptions are not always inconsistent, they nevertheless attest to the fact that the dimensions of the proposed new subspecialty are by no means clear cut. These conceptions range all the way from the idea that community psychiatry means bringing psychiatric techniques and treatments to the indigent in the community, to the notion that community psychiatry should involve the education of policemen, teachers, public health nurses, politicians, and junior executives in mental hygiene principles. A mere listing of some of the conceptions of what has been placed under the community psychiatry umbrella will give a further notion of this uncertainty. Community psychiatry has been regarded as encompassing: (1) the community base mental hospital; (2) short-term mental hospitalization; (3) attempts to move the chronically hospitalized patient and return him to the community; (4) integration of various community health services; (5) psychiatric counseling and services to nonpsychiatric institutions such as schools, police departments, industries, and the like; (6) development of devices for maintaining mental patients in the community; (7) reorganization and administration of community mental health programs; and finally, (8) establishment of auxiliary services to community mental hospitals, such as outpatient clinics, day hospitals, night hospitals, home psychiatric visits, and the utilization of auxiliary psychiatric personnel in treatment programs.[3]

Perhaps we can come close to what someone visualizes as the content of community psychiatry by quoting an announcement of an opening for a fellowship in community psychiatry in Minnesota. The announcement described the program as follows: "One year of diversified training and experience, including all aspects of community organization, consultation, and training techniques, administration, research and mass communication media." Such a psychiatric residency program certainly represents a great difference from the more traditional training program and points to a type of training that might be more fitting for a person who wants to specialize in community organization.

There is no clearer support for this conception than Leonard Duhl's paper[4] where he discusses the training problems for community psychiatry. In this paper he speaks of three contracts that the psychiatrist has, the traditional one with the patient, the more infrequent one with the family, and the still more infrequent one with the community. In connection with his community contract, according to Duhl, the psychiatrist states: "I will try to lower the rate of illness and maximize the health of this population." Duhl continues, and I quote, because the direction is most significant.

> In preparing psychiatrists for these broadened contracts, a new set of skills must be communicated. For example, he must learn how to be consultant to a community, an institution, or a group without being patient-oriented. Rather, he must have the community's needs in central focus. He must be prepared for situations where he is expected to contribute to planning for services and programs, both in his field and in others, that are related: what information is needed: how it is gathered; what resources are available, and so forth. Epidemiology, survey research, and planning skills must be passed on to him. He must be prepared to find that people in other fields such as the legislature often affect a program more than his profession does. He must find himself at home in the world of economics, political science, politics, planning, and all forms of social action.[5]

While these remarks by Bernard and Duhl may not represent any final statement as to what community psychiatry will become, they point to a probable direction that this newest addition to psychiatric subspecialties may take. However, so many uncertainties, unresolved issues, and hidden assumptions are in this conception of the community psychiatrist as a person skilled in the techniques of social action that it is difficult to determine where it will be most effective to start the analysis, with the role of the psychiatrist or with the nature of the community.

Perhaps sociologists can garner some small satisfaction in the fact that the psychiatrist finally has discovered the community—something that the sociologist has been studying and reporting on for over half a century in the United States. However, once the psychiatrist makes this discovery, he must ask himself what he can do with it in light of his professional task, how the discovery will affect his traditional professional role, and how working on or in the community structure can improve the mental health level of the people. Now it seems that those leaders of psychiatry who are proposing this new subspecialty imply several things at the same time and are vague about all of them. In one form or another they seem to be saying the following:

1. We psychiatrists must know the community and learn how to work with the various groups and social strata composing it so that we can help to secure and organize the necessary psychiatric facilities that will serve to maximize the treatment potential for the mentally ill.

2. We must know the community because the community is composed of families which, through the interaction of their members, evolve those events and processes that in a given context have a pathic effect upon some of the persons who compose them.
3. We must know the community in order to develop more effective methods of treatment at the "collective level," to eliminate mentally disorganizing social relationships, and to achieve a type of community organization that is most conducive to the preservation of mental health.
4. We must know the community if we are ever to make any headway in the prevention of mental illness. For we hold that in multiple groups, families, and social institutions which compose the community there are numerous unhealthy interpersonal relationships, pathological attitudes and beliefs, cultural conflicts and tensions, and unhealthy child-training practices that make for the development of mental and emotional disturbances in the person.

An analysis of our first implication shows that no new burden is placed upon the psychiatrist, but it merely emphasizes his role as a citizen—a role that, like any person in the society, he always has had. It merely emphasizes that the psychiatrist will take a more active part in working with other professionals in the community such as lawyers, teachers, social workers, ministers, labor leaders, and businessmen in achieving an organization of psychiatric facilities that will maximize the therapeutic potential in a given community. To be sure, it means that in working with such persons and groups he will contribute his own professional knowledge and insights in the attempt to obtain and to organize the psychiatric facilities in such a manner as to achieve a maximum therapeutic potential. Thus, this is hardly a new role for the psychiatrist. It only becomes sharper at this moment in history when a social change in the care and treatment of the mentally ill is impending, namely, a shift from a situation that emphasized the removal of the mental patient from the community to one that attempts to deal with him in the community and family setting and to keep his ties with these social structures active and intact.

The second implication is routine in light of the orientation of much of contemporary psychiatry. Here attention is merely called to the theory that stresses the atypical qualities of the family drama to provide an etiological push for the development of the several psychoneuroses, character disorders, adult behavior disturbances, and in certain instances psychotic reactions. Thus it follows that to change or correct the condition found in the person, some attention must be paid to the family as a collectivity, in order to grasp and then modify those attitudes, behavior patterns, identifications, and emotional attachments that supposedly have a pathogenic effect on the family members. From the focus on the family, the concern then extends to the larger community in an attempt to discover the degree to which the family is integrated in or alienated from it.

However, it is in the third implication that many probing questions arise. For here the conception is implicit that the community is the patient, and consequently the necessity arises to develop techniques that can be used in treating the community toward the end of supplementing the traditional one-to-one psychiatric relationship. This position also implies a certain etiological view, namely, that within the texture of those institutional arrangements that make up the community, there exist dysfunctional processes, subcultures with unhealthy value complexes, specific institutional tensions, various ideological conflicts with age, sex, ethnic, racial, and political bases, occasional cultural crises, and an increasing tempo of social change that provide a pathogenic social environment in their functional interrelationships. Thus, when these elements are incorporated into the experiences of persons, especially during their early and adolescent years, abnormal traits, attitudes, thought processes, and behavior patterns emerge. In a theoretical vein, this is the Merton[6] paradigm wherein he attempts to show diverse modes of adaptation that arise as a result of the various patterns of discrepancy between institutional means and cultural goals.

The influence of the social milieu in shaping, organizing, and integrating the personality structure has of course been recognized for a long time. What is not so clear, however, is the manner in which such knowledge can be utilized in working at the community level to treat the mental and emotional maladjustments that continually appear. In addition, the nature and function of those factors in the social milieu that contribute to the production of bona fide psychotics are by no means established.

These issues point to some very pressing queries: What are the possible techniques that can be developed to treat the "collectivity"? Why do psychiatrists think that it is possible to treat the "collectivity" when a marked uncertainty with respect to the treatment and cure of the individual case still exists? What causes the psychiatrist to think that if he advances certain techniques for treating the "collectivity," they will have community acceptance? If he begins to "treat" a group through discussions in order to develop personal insights, what assurances does he have that the results will be psychologically beneficial to the persons? Does the psychiatrist know how to organize a community along mentally hygienic lines, and if he does, what evidence does he have that such an organization will be an improvement over the existing one? In what institutional setting or cultural milieu would the psychiatrist expect to begin in order to move toward more healthy social relationships in the community? These are serious questions, and I raise them with reference to the concept that the community is the patient.

If a psychiatrist thinks that he can organize the community to become a more healthy entity, I suggest that he run for some public office. This would certainly add to his experience and give him some conception as to whether or not the community is ready to be moved in the direction that he regards as mentally hygienic. If he should decide on such a step, he will be successful to the extent that he jokingly refers to himself as a "head shrinker" and that he becomes acceptable as "one of the boys." But if he does, he functions as an independent citizen, in harmony with our democratic ethos, bringing his professional knowledge to bear on the goal he has set for himself and his constituents. However, successful or not, he will certainly achieve new insight concerning the complexity involved in treating the community as the patient.

While I have poked at this proposition from the standpoint of politics, let me consider it with respect to education. If this becomes the medium by which the pathology of the community is to be arrested, one can assume that it means adding to and raising the quality of the educational system in the community. Psychiatric information with respect to signs and symptoms, the desirability of early treatment, the natural character of mental illness, the therapeutic benefits of new drugs, and the correct mental hygiene principles of child training has been disseminated not only through usual community lectures and formal educational channels, but also by means of the mass media—radio, television, newspapers, and slick magazines. I hasten to add, however, that this may not be to the advantage of the community, for it may do nothing else but raise the level of anxiety among certain middle-class persons who, when they read an article on the correct procedure for bringing up children, realize that they have done all the wrong things. Also, the media are frequently sources of misinformation and sometimes imply a promise that psychiatry cannot fulfill.

Further, I observe that in this proposal for a community psychiatry, the psychiatrist seems to be enmeshed in the same cultural vortex as is the professor. It is becoming fashionable for a professor to measure his success by having hardly any contact with students—he is too busy on larger undertakings, research, consultation, conferences, and the like. Likewise, some psychiatrists think that they have arrived if they have no contact with patients. For example, I have heard of one psychiatrist who has not seen a patient for several years—he spends his time educating teachers, nurses, policemen, businessmen, and the laity in psychiatric principles.

The third and fourth implications of the new focus provided by community psychiatry are closely related: each position partially views the structures and processes of the community as containing certain etiological elements that make for the development of certain types of mental and emotional illness. However, the third implication, as we have shown, points to the development of treatment techniques on the collective level, while the fourth emphasizes that knowledge of the community is essential if mental illness is ever to be prevented.

There is no doubt that the word "prevention" falling on the ears of well-intentioned Americans is just what the doctor ordered. It is so hopeful that no one, I am sure, will deny that if we can prevent our pathologies this is far better than sitting back and waiting for them to develop. But, of course, there is a catch. How are we going to take the first preventive actions if we are still uncertain about the causes of mental disorders? How do we even know where to cut into a community's round of life? And if we did cut in, what assurance would we have that the results might not be completely opposite of those anticipated? Of course there is always secondary prevention—that is, directing our efforts to prevent a recurrence of illness in persons who have once been sick. This is a laudable goal, but in connection with mental and emotional disturbances we are still uncertain of the success of our original treatment.

PREVENTION OF BEHAVIORAL PATHOLOGY —SOME PREVIOUS EFFORTS

There is no doubt that the possibility of prevention is something that will continue to intrigue us for years to come. Therefore, it is reasonable to take a look at several other programs that, while not exclusively oriented toward the treatment of the community, have been launched with the hope of preventing the occurrence of certain unacceptable behavior on the part of the members of a community. I cite two experiments which are widely known with respect to the prevention of delinquency.

The first is Kobrin's statement concerning the twenty-five year assessment of the Chicago Area

Project.[7] Kobrin has presented a straightforward, modest, and sophisticated account of the accumulated experience provided by this project and its efforts to bring about greater control of delinquency in certain areas of Chicago. This project has been significant on several counts, but in my judgment its greatest significance is that it helped initiate various types of community organizational programs that logically proceeded from an empirically developed theory of delinquency. This theory, in general, viewed delinquency primarily as a "breakdown of the machinery of spontaneous social control." The theory stressed that delinquency was adaptive behavior by adolescents in their peer groups, and represented efforts to achieve meaningful and respected adult roles, "unaided by the older generation and under the influence of criminal models for whom the intercity areas furnish a haven." This theory, in turn, rests upon certain sociological postulates which emphasize that the development and control of conduct are determined by the network of primary relationships in which one's daily existence is embedded.

This experiment was significant because this theory of delinquency provided a rationalization for going into certain areas of the community and seeking persons who were interested in receiving a higher level of welfare for themselves and their children. The results of this experiment are relevant to those who advocate the preventive function of a community psychiatry: not only was there difficulty in determining what actually had been accomplished in the way of delinquency prevention but there was also a difficulty in assessing the experience in relation to community welfare.

In his opening sentence, Kobrin has stated this problem most cogently:

> The Chicago Area Project shares with other delinquency prevention programs the difficulty of measuring its success in a simple and direct manner. At bottom this difficulty rests on the fact that such programs, as efforts to intervene in the life of a person, a group, or a community, cannot, by their very nature, constitute more than a subsidiary element in changing the fundamental and sweeping forces which create the problems of groups and of persons or which shape human personality. Decline in rates of delinquents—the only conclusive way to evaluate delinquency prevention—may reflect influences unconnected with those of organized programs and are difficult to define and measure.[8]

The point here is that in a carefully detailed plan based upon an empirical theory, it is difficult to determine what has been achieved. If this is true with respect to delinquent behavior with its roots deeply enmeshed in the network of social relationships, how much more difficult it will be in the field of psychiatry to make an assessment in preventive efforts, where we are much more uncertain of the etiology of those who appear in psychiatric offices, clinics, and hospitals.

The well-known Cambridge-Summerville Youth Study[9] provides a second example of a delinquency prevention program. While this study did not focus upon the entire community, but rather on certain individuals, it did proceed from a conception of the relationship between a person's needs and a treatment framework for administering to those needs. In this study, an attempt was made to provide a warm, human, and continuing relationship between an assigned counselor and a sample of delinquents, and to deny this relationship from another comparably matched sample. With most of the boys in the treatment group, this relationship lasted for approximately eight years. At the conclusion of the experiment, the attempt to assess the results proved mainly negative. The number of boys in the treatment group who appeared before the crime prevention bureau of the police department was slightly larger than the number of boys making such appearances in the control group. The only positive note was that the boys in the control group were somewhat more active as recidivists than were the boys in the treatment group.

Although the results of this study are inconclusive and tell us nothing in particular about the communities to which these boys were reacting, they do document the failure of one type of relationship therapy to reduce delinquency. While these results provide no final word, they do point up the necessity for the various techniques in psychiatry to acquire a far greater effectiveness than they now possess before starting to operate on a community level, where there will be a great deal of fumbling in the dark before knowing exactly what to do.

It seems most appropriate, in light of the task envisioned for community psychiatry, to call attention to the professional excitement that was engendered when the Commonwealth Fund inaugurated a child-guidance program in 1922. The Child Guidance Clinic was hailed as a step that eventually would have far-reaching consequences. For who saw fit at that time, in light of certain prevailing theories and the optimism provided by the cultural ethos of the United States, to deny that, if emotional, mental, and behavioral disturbances were ever to be arrested and prevented at the adult level, it would be necessary to arrest these tendencies at their incipient stage, namely, in childhood. This all appears most logical and reasonable. Forty years after the opening of the first child guidance clinic, such clinics are to be found in almost every state, and they are very much utilized as evidenced by the long waiting lists. Nevertheless, not only does juvenile delinquency remain a continuing community problem, but also the adult incidence rates of at least the major psychoses appear also approximately constant during this period, especially if the study by Goldhamer and Marshall[10] is accepted as valid.

I cite these three different kinds of experience primarily to emphasize the necessity for reviewing our past efforts in attacking certain behavioral problems at a community level, and also to point to some of the difficulties inherent in any proposal that emphasizes the development of psychiatric treatment techniques for the "collective level."

THE WIDENING DEFINITION OF MENTAL ILLNESS

Efforts to carve out the subspecialty of community psychiatry take place in a cultural atmosphere which has seen a definite attempt to widen the definition of mental illness. This is shown by the tendency in our society to place any recognized behavior deviant into the sick role. By doing this, we not only supposedly understand them, but we can also point to therapies which will be appropriate for their treatment. Thus, in the past two decades, the following have often been placed in the sick role: delinquents, sex offenders, alcoholics, drug addicts, beatniks, Communists, the racially prejudiced, and in fact, practically all persons who do not fit into the prevailing togetherness that we like to think characterizes middle-class American life. The danger here is that we only add to our state of confusion, because the line between who is sick and who is well increasingly becomes a waving, uncertain one. Thus, we appear to constantly move the cutting point toward the end of the continuum that would include persons who, in some subcultural milieus, are accepted as normal.

There is much current statistical evidence that supports this notion of a widening definition for mental illness. For example, if one compares the community epidemiological surveys of mental illness in the

1930's with those of the 1950's one is struck with the
fact that four to five times more cases are reported
in the latter years.[11] In my own epidemiological
study of schizophrenia, I have examined many
epidemiological studies from all over the world, and
have noted: the great differences that are reported
with respect to total mental disorders in the surveys,
a marked decrease in the differences between the
surveys when only psychoses are reported, and a still
further decrease in the rate variations when the reports are based only upon schizophrenia. In the latter case, the variations are slight and all of the rates
are quite close together. One might point to the Mid-
town Manhattan survey[12] where two psychiatrists reviewed symptom schedules on a sample population
as collected by field workers and found that approximately 80 percent of the sample were suffering from
some type of psychiatric symptom. This extreme figure can be contrasted with the 20 percent reported
as incapacitated. Providing adequate psychiatric services for even the latter figure would place an impossible burden on any community.

Several factors help to explain this widening
definition of mental illness, so apparent during the
past two decades. One factor, of course, has been the
adaptation of psychiatry to office practice following
World War II.[13] Another factor is the mounting frustration resulting from failures to achieve therapeutic
results with bona fide psychotics, and a widening of
the psychiatric net to include those persons with minor emotional disturbances who are more responsive
to existing treatment techniques. These people are

suffering from what has been termed "problems of living," and they do not represent the bona fide mentally ill cases.[14] In this connection, it is interesting to note that George W. Albee stated at an American Medical Association meeting in Chicago:

> What we clearly do not need more of in the mental health profession are people who go into private practice of psychotherapy with middle-aged neurotics in high income suburbs. While there are humanitarian and ethical reasons for offering all the help we possibly can to individuals afflicted with mental disorders, it seems unlikely that we will ever have the manpower to offer individual care on any kind of manageable ratio of therapists to sufferers.[15]

In light of Albee's observation, it is instructive to note Paul Hoch's evaluation[16] of the therapeutic accomplishments of mental health clinics in New York State. With respect to psychotherapeutic techniques, he states:

> I do not mean to deny that psychotherapy brings relief to those suffering from emotional disorders or that it may not be the treatment of choice in certain cases. What I am questioning is the preoccupation with intensive psychotherapy in clinics which are part of the community health program. After more than fifty years of this utilization we still have no proof of its effectiveness, of its superiority over other forms of treatment or even [that] a long term is better than brief psychotherapy.

He goes on to point out that even though 30,000 patients were released from the state hospital in the previous year, only 8 percent of the cases who were terminated by psychiatric clinics came from inpatient facilities. He also notes that the volume of patients being treated in state hospitals is greater than ever before, in spite of an almost unanimous need to develop alternative care. His evidence supports this contention of a widening definition of mental illness, implying that the outpatient clinics are not treating cases who are likely to need hospital care, but are treating numerous cases who are experiencing emotional problems. These are primarily concerned with the daily round of human existence and can never be completely eliminated except in a societal utopia. One conclusion appears inescapable—the more clinics, the more patients. In addition, this widening definition of mental illness has served as fuel for the development of the idea of a community psychiatry.

HISTORICAL AND CULTURAL INFLUENCES

Every historian recognizes the problem of how far back one should go in enumerating events which helped to shape the present because every historical event is both a consequence of some previous happening and a cause of something that will take place in the future. However, I begin my history of the proposal for a community psychiatry with the accumulated psychiatric experience which came out of World War II. Psychiatric experience during the war showed that a large number of inductees were afflicted with various types of neuropsychiatric disorders. This finding was reported by Dr. William Menninger, head of psychiatric services of the U.S. Armed Forces. In a book dealing with his war experiences, he also anticipated the uses to which psychiatry might be put in meeting new problems and tensions that were arising in American society and throughout the world. Menninger[17] asks if, after the war, psychiatry is to continue its preoccupation with the end results of mental disease, or "to discover how it can contribute to the problems of the average man and to the larger social issues in which he is involved." Thus, Menninger anticipated that the new role for psychiatry would be expanded to deal with family problems, industrial conflict, community conflict, and in fact, any situation where conflict, difficulties, and tensions arise between people. Thus, the publication of this work seemed to play a role in turning psychiatry away from its traditional concerns and in directing its attention to problems of the community.

The work of Menninger, Thompson,[18] and others tended to anticipate a more positive and frontal attack upon mental health problems in American society. The writings of these men set the stage for the passage of the National Mental Health Act in 1948 which has played a significant role in stimulating professional training, research, and treatment programs in psychiatry and its allied fields. After passage of this act, which raised mental health to the status of a public health problem, numerous events followed swiftly. Certainly the new monies available through the Federal Government and foundations made it possible for scholars from all over the United States and Europe to meet more often to deal with specific problems in the mental health field. This exchange of scholars acquainted psychiatric workers in the United States with the various programs and plans that were being carried on in Europe for handling mental health problems, such as Querido's program for community psychiatry in Amsterdam, the development of the open-door hospital in England, auxiliary psychiatric units such as night hospitals and day hospitals, rehabilitation houses, and various kinds of industrial units to train mental convalescents for jobs. All of these developments proved most exciting and interesting, stimulated thinking, broke through conventional and traditional concepts of the past, and paved the way for taking many new looks at how we could more adequately treat the mentally ill in order more quickly to return them to their families and communities.

In fact, these developments began to undercut various conceptions of chronicity, and we recognized that hospitalization for mental illness need not be a life-time affair. We should also call attention to research on the mental hospital conducted by social scientists which provided a rationale for the hospital as a therapeutic community, a development that Maxwell Jones[19] in his work in England has already anticipated. However, studies during the 1950's by Stanton and Schwartz,[20] Dunham and Weinberg,[21] Belknap,[22] John and Elaine Cumming,[23] and W. Caudill[24] increasingly began to pose the issue as to whether the therapeutic community could be considered a real factor in the treatment process. These studies further called attention to the rigid traditional structure of the state hospital and how it actually contained within itself those cultural forms that tended to discourage patients toward moving to a level of acceptable behavior. Then came the report of a Joint Commission on Mental Illness and Health[25] in 1961, along with the Surgeon General's recommendation in 1962 that the states explore a more complete utilization of all community resources dealing with the mentally ill to achieve a maximum in the prevention and treatment of such illnesses. And as a final stimulus came the speech of the late President Kennedy[26] to Congress in October, 1963, in which he outlined a broad program with respect to community-centered hospitals, research, and training, covering both mental illness and mental retardation.

In the above account I have attempted a cursory examination of the central historical events that have led to the development of community psychiatry. However, in a broader perspective, these events can be regarded as the consequences of the cultural forces embodied in certain beliefs and traditions that are deeply embedded in the texture of American society. In a sense, the emergence of community psychiatry as a subspecialty of psychiatry is a reflection of the cherished American belief that we can solve all of our problems if we can just discover the key by means of the scientific methodology at our disposal. The ever-multiplying programs of health insurance during the past twenty years have also laid an economic foundation, making it possible to bring mental patients out in the open instead of hiding them away as we had done in the past. Under these conditions, the essential qualities of American culture, individualism, optimism, humanism, and equalitarianism have merely provided the additional push for the emergence of community psychiatry.

Some Hidden Aspects for the Future Role of Psychiatry

In this account, I have pointed to the several conceptions which seem to be implied in the development of a community psychiatry. I have emphasized that tying community psychiatry with the several evolving plans throughout the country to reorganize mental health facilities in order to maximize treatment potential is a significant move. While there is the question whether community psychiatry extends beyond current psychiatric practices, there may be a gain in identifying the psychiatrist more closely with the different community services and breaking down the isolation in which both the psychoanalytic practitioner and the hospital practicing psychiatrist have been enmeshed. This would not only move the psychiatrist closer to the patient, but what is more important, closer to the entire network of interpersonal relationships of the family and the community in which the patient lives.

However, it is the other visions that have been held up for community psychiatry wherein, I think, as I have indicated, great difficulties are in the offing. Here I am most skeptical concerning the adequacy of our knowledge to develop significant techniques for treating social collectivities or for developing techniques on the community level that will really result in a reduction of mental disturbances in the community. It seems that such expectations are likely to move the psychiatrist still further from the more bona fide cases of mental illnesses in the community. Much of his effort will be spent in dealing with noncritical cases. This trend has already been going on for some time, as I indicated in discussing the widening definition of mental illness. Until we have more indication that minor emotional disturbances are likely to develop into more serious types of mental disturbances, we will be dissipating much of our collective psychiatric efforts.

Then, too, there is another hidden aspect of these projected conceptions of community psychiatry which deserves careful exploration. I refer to the implication that the psychiatrist will be able to move into the ongoing power structure of a community. The profession must confront the issue as to whether its effectiveness will be lessened or increased if some of its members should succeed in obtaining roles within the power structure of the community. Here, I would suggest that the psychiatrist would find himself in a system where his professional effectiveness would be considerably reduced because he would be involved in a series of mutual obligations and expectations in relation to the other persons composing the power structure. He would thus lose the role that in general characterizes the professional in other areas, that as adviser and consultant with respect to any psychiatric problems or issues that the groups, institutions, and associations of the community confront. In becoming part of the power structure, he is likely to lose more than he gains: that is, his gains would be in respect to power, personal prestige, and recognition but his losses would be in the growing rustiness of his diagnostic and therapeutic skills with patients.

Another implication of these aspects of community psychiatry is that psychiatrists are being pushed in a direction not entirely of their own making. The national efforts and monies that are being directed to states and communities for the reorganization of mental health facilities have engendered a high degree of excitement among professional social workers, mental health educators, psychiatric nurses, and numerous well-intentioned persons who see new professional opportunities for service and careers. Thus, the psychiatrist is led to think, because of these pressures, that he should learn new skills in order to provide the required leadership to the various professionals who are planning to work toward this new vision of maximizing treatment potential in the community for the mentally ill.

Finally, there is the implication that psychiatry is being utilized to move us closer in the direction of the welfare state. This may not be undesirable in itself, but it seems most essential that psychiatrists should be aware of the role that they are asked to play. We can anticipate that while the doctor-patient relationship will still be paramount in most medical practice, the psychiatrist is likely to move into unforeseen roles which will be required by the new structural organization of psychiatric facilities with the proposal for a community psychiatry. In such new roles, psychiatrists may become agents for social control, thus sacrificing the main task for which their education has fitted them.

In this paper, I have attempted to show the link between community psychiatry and the new evolving community mental health programs. While one can see in this linkage a most significant development, I am somewhat skeptical toward those emphases in community psychiatry which aim at the development of treatment techniques on the community level. In discussing the widening definition of mental illness, I have tried to show that this is one of the crucial factors that has accounted for this movement toward a new type of psychiatric specialty. I have seen, in this widening definition, an opportunity to overcome a frustration that engulfs psychiatrists with respect to their inability to make much therapeutic headway with traditional mental cases. Finally, I have attempted to consider some of the hidden implications for psychiatry in the proposal for this new psychiatric specialty.

REFERENCES

1. V. Bernard, "Some Interrelationships of Training for Community Psychiatry, Community Mental Health Programs and Research in Social Psychiatry," in *Proceedings of Third World Congress of Psychiatry,* 3 (Montreal, Canada: McGill University and University of Toronto Press, 1961): 67–71.
2. S. E. Goldston, "Training in Community Psychiatry: Survey Report of Medical School Department of Psychiatry," *American J. Psychiat.,* 120, (Feb 1964): 789–792.
3. *Ibid.*
4. L. J. Duhl, "Problems in Training Psychiatric Residents in Community Psychiatry," paper read before the Institute on Training in Community Psychiatry at the University of California, mimeographed, Fall–Winter, 1963–1964, p. 6.
5. *Ibid.*
6. R. K. Merton, "Social Structure and Anomie," in *Social Theory and Social Structure,* (Glencoe, Ill: The Free Press, 1949), pp. 125–150.
7. S. Kobrin, "Chicago Area Project—25-Year Assessment," *Ann. Amer. Acad. Political Soc. Sci.* 322 (March 1959): 20–29.
8. *Ibid.*
9. E. Powers and H. Witmer, *Experiment in Prevention of Delinquency,* (New York: Columbia University Press, 1951).
10. H. Goldhamer and A. Marshall, *Psychoses and Civilization,* (Glencoe, Ill: The Free Press, 1953).

11. R. J. Plunkett and J. E. Gordon, *Epidemiology and Mental Illness,* (New York: Basic Books, 1960), p. 90.
12. L. Srole et al. *Mental Health in Metropolis: Midtown Manhattan Study,* vol. 1, (New York: McGraw-Hill, 1962).
13. W. E. Barton, "Presidential Address—Psychiatry in Transition," *Amer. J. Psychiat.,* 119, (July 1962): 1–15.
14. T. S. Szasz, *Myth of Mental Illness: Foundations of Theory of Personal Conduct* (New York: Paul B. Hoeber, Inc., Medical Division Harper & Brothers, 1961).
15. Paul H. Hoch, "Therapeutic Accomplishments of Mental Health Clinics," *Ment. Hygiene News,* (June, 1963): 1–3.
16. *Ibid.*
17. W. Menninger, *Psychiatry in a Troubled World,* (New York: The Macmillan Company, 1948), chap. 13.
18. C. B. Thompson, *"Psychiatry and Social Crisis,"* *J. Clin. Psychopath.* 7 (April 1946): 697–711.
19. M. Jones, *Therapeutic Community: New Treatment Method in Psychiatry,* (New York: Basic Books, 1953).
20. A. Stanton and M. S. Schwartz, *The Mental Hospital: A Study of Institutional Participation,* in *Psychiatric Illness and Treatment,* (New York: Basic Books, 1954).
21. H. W. Dunham and S. K. Weinberg, *Culture of State Mental Hospital,* (Detroit: The Wayne State University Press, 1960).

22. I. Belknap, *Human Problems of State Mental Hospital,* (New York: Blakiston, Medical Division McGraw-Hill Book Co., 1956).
23. J. Cumming and E. Cumming, *Closed Ranks: Experiment in Mental Health Education,* (Cambridge, Massachusetts: Harvard University Press, Commonwealth Fund, 1957).
24. W. Caudill, *Psychiatric Hospital as a Small Society,* (Cambridge, Massachusetts: Harvard University Press, 1958).
25. Joint Commission on Mental Illness and Health, *Action for Mental Health,* (New York: Basic Books, 1961), p. 333.
26. J. F. Kennedy, "Message From President of United States Relative to Mental Illness and Mental Retardation," February 5, 1963, *Amer. J. Psychiat.* 120 (February 1964) 729–737.

—6—

Neglected Realities in the Development of Community Psychiatry

The increasing prominence of the psychiatric profession in all areas of our national life suggests the necessity to explore the implications of such ubiquity. One possible exploration is to take a fresh look at community psychiatry, the new subspecialty of general psychiatry, by analyzing the theoretical model upon which it has been grafted; by examining some of the facts of mental illness seemingly forgotten by its advocates; and finally, by portraying some problems in the process in which the new community psychiatrists will be and are being involved.[1]

This new psychiatric specialty that is taking shape is, in great measure, attributed to the pioneering of Duhl[2] and to the several symposia on community psychiatry that took place in various parts of the

country during the past decade. This new specialty
is further seen in the recent report of a committee of
the Group for the Advancement of Psychiatry,[3]
which attempts to deal with the kind of education
that a community psychiatrist should receive without coming to any clear focus as to how the subspecialty is to be described and delimited. This
particular committee has naturally been concerned
with the possible relationships between community
psychiatry and clinical and psychoanalytically oriented psychiatry. As might be expected, the committee recognized that it is not an either/or matter and
that dynamic psychiatry is being not replaced but
enriched. And finally, after stating that "the proper
role of social psychiatry is to treat the community
and not the individual patient," the report continues
by saying that "community psychiatry is considered
as supplementary to the psychiatrist's core skill, his
one-to-one clinical approach."

Nevertheless, in spite of these apologetics, the
report attempts to spell out the proper training for
a third-, fourth- or fifth-year resident aiming to
become a community psychiatrist. The kind of
knowledge that the committee advocates would include human ecology, epidemiological studies of
mental illness and social system theory, along with
several weeks of field work in various kinds of agencies such as courts, industrial organizations, family
agencies, schools, public health departments, health
departments of labor unions and the like. While
these subjects are emphasized by the committee's
report, various ongoing programs in departments of

psychiatry offer other special courses such as the design and conduct of surveys, community organization, mental health planning, experimental design, preventive psychiatry, community processes, legal aspects of community mental health and advanced statistics. However, when all of these things are added up, the theoretical underpinnings for community psychiatry are to be found in comtemporary sociology: structural-functional theory or social system theory.

System Models in Community Psychiatry

These various attempts to delineate the subject matter of community psychiatry point to the necessity of examining the theoretical models upon which this new subspecialty is based. One such social system model, the rational type, projects an organized structure of separate parts, each one of which can be individually manipulated and modified with a view toward bringing about an increased efficiency of the total structure. In contrast, a natural system model is also made up of different parts, but the stress is placed on their interdependence in such a way that any change that is introduced with respect to any one part will have ramifying influences throughout the entire organized system. Each of these models can be regarded as having evolved from simpler social structures and often are viewed as the most complex type of organization in nature. These models, in the hands of sociologists, have been utilized to point up researchable hypotheses, to guide empirical studies and to provide for more meaningful interpretations of empirical findings.

There is the further implication that these models constitute the social-ecological environment for individuals serving as units or cells. Thus from this perspective the evolving system, if it develops too much disequilibrium, can build certain types of mental and behavioral pathology into the various individuals composing it. While recent sociological theory has developed a greater precision in the intellectual construction of these models, their roots are deeply embedded in the history of Western social thought.

Further, it should be noted that these models visualize the possibility of the development of a social engineering. In other words, they seem to hold out the promise that if social knowledge can be developed in one area of the social system, represented by the model, say, for example, the social class structure, then it would seem to follow that such knowledge might be applied to bring about changes in the class structure in the direction that might enhance the functional utility of the entire system. In addition, it might be pointed out, that this possibility is particulary attractive to western man, and especially so in the United States, where the ideal has always been held out that eventually he will master his environment if not his own soul. By these remarks I do not tend to negate the possibility of any type of social engineering utilizing a body of tested social knowledge. But I do intend to challenge any social engineering effort when our knowledge is vague and uncertain and when there is no tested knowledge about intervention possibilities.[4]

The position can be asserted that these theoretical models, upon which community psychiatry is based, lend themselves to various kinds of empirical work which in turn lead to the output of objective and verifiable knowledge that can be transmitted. Thus, the model is a natural science one where objective and verifiable knowledge form the basis of our developing and advanced technology. As it is in the physical sciences, so, by this path, it will be in the social sciences. In other words, the promise is there that the objective and verifiable knowledge of the social sciences can be transmitted to the scientifically trained psychiatrist whereby he will be able to go into the community and/or various institutional structures and apply such knowledge in ways that are advantageous with respect to agreed-upon ends in order to bring about a more healthy functioning of the total social system which, in turn, will make for more harmonious and healthy personalities as they develop within the social system.

The work that the community psychiatrist will be asked to do has been visualized not only by these theoretical models, but also by the GAP Report and the numerous papers by Duhl. Let me quote a paragraph from this report that not only describes the work of the community psychiatrist but also gives implicit support to our rational model of a social system.

The psychiatrist's investment of himself in the organization increases and he becomes interested in personnel not referred to him. These personnel may be characterized by low productivity, absenteeism or other discernably aberrant behavior traceable to personality or situational disorders. Soon his attention is drawn to all members of the organization who may not be functioning optimally. As his relationship with administrative personnel becomes closer he is asked to help with problems of selection, placement and promotion. Now the psychiatrist is making judgments about relatively healthy persons and, through his screening techniques, is influencing the quality of persons that make up the organization. Increasing demands within this relatively stable system require modifications of his initial model of functioning. He begins to realize that when mental disorder occurs there are a variety of possibilities available for modifying interpersonal relationships and re-establishing a healthier equilibrium.[5]

Three facets of this statement are noteworthy. First, the community psychiatrist will supposedly work closely with the administrative personnel of an organization in order to achieve optimal functioning. The heart of the problem is not touched upon, namely, how this is to be measured and what standards are to be employed. Secondly, it is implied that by modifying interpersonal relationships and reestablishing a healthier equilibrium in the organization it may be possible to prevent mental disorder. Finally, the community psychiatrist is assigned the task of screening personnel and thus, influencing the quality of persons who make up the organization.

One can only wonder if the committee had any awareness of the implications of what it was requiring of the community psychiatrist. Does the community psychiatrist intend to supplant the ordinary selection process that goes on in the organization? In dealing with these so-called healthy personalities, what kind of criteria is he going to utilize? Finally, what about the relatively healthy persons who are eliminated from the organization by the screening techniques of the psychiatrist? What is likely to happen when these persons discover that they were refused employment because some psychiatrist decided that they were unfit? I am, of course, referring here only to the use of the psychiatrist in selecting employees and not to his already established role of treating those persons in the organization who are referred to him or seek his help for some emotional problem.

Some already object to the wide use of tests that have been developed and utilized by psychologists in personnel selection. At least these tests have some objective character to them and are generally used in connection with an interview with the applicant. They have also proven of value in such large-scale undertakings as military induction when judgments of many people have to be made in a short period of time. Furthermore, the objective character of these tests is such that they do not have the stigma at-

tached to them that may be generated if a psychiatrist does the screening.

In much the same vein as the screening proposal, Duhl has projected some of the new tasks for
the community psychiatrist:

> As I view it, there are six levels of preventive
> measures which can be taken: 1. The general
> promotion of mental health by increasing the
> strength and toleration to stress of individuals
> and communities in a non-specific manner . . .
> 2. The elimination of deprivations . . . 3. The
> interruption of the pathogenic trains of events
> by diminishing or eliminating stress which lead
> to disaster . . . 4. The prevention of major men-
> tal illness, delinquency, drug addiction, and so
> forth, by early detection and referral to avail-
> able community resources . . . 5. The arrest of
> illness by treatment, and the subsequent
> rehabilitation of the ill through coordinated ac-
> tivities of private practitioners, institutions,
> clinics, and the community . . . 6. The preven-
> tion of permanent disability by the treatment of
> psychological disturbances. . . .
> We are becoming increasingly aware of the
> changed world in which we live. . . . For exam-
> ple, we can look at adolescence not only as a
> period of psycho-social growth, but as an eco-
> nomic market to be catered to and developed,
> thus leading to tremendous pressures on the
> individual to conform. . . . The psychiatrist, too,
> must look at the total ecology of man and de-
> cide where are the best points of intervention.
> . . . A simple awareness of the impact of commu-

nity decisions on people can often be the key to maintaining or replacing these supports. . . . (Neighborhood fraternal organization, the friendly bartender or grocer, the corner cop). The psychiatrist must truly be a political personage in the best sense of the word. He must play a role in *controlling* the environment which man has created.[6]

I recognize that Duhl is attempting to sense some of the needs of our emerging social order, but I cannot help but point out that there is a big gap between the theory underlying his proposals and the applications of that theory to the solution of some community mental health problems. For example, his six levels of preventive measures have been reiterated, as Duhl well knows, in various contexts by numerous professionals from time to time. Does the psychiatric profession have in its possession the techniques and the skills necessary to achieve the promises implied by these preventive measures? How is the psychiatrist to go about the task of increasing the strength and toleration to stress of individuals? What evidence exists that major mental illness, delinquency, or drug addiction can be arrested by early detection and referral? For example delinquency, by its very nature, is often early detected. But early identification has hardly helped us to achieve prevention. What evidence exists that permanent disabilities are necessarily eliminated by the treatment of psychological disturbance? And how is the psychiatrist going to go about eliminating deprivations which are both cultural and economic products that are tightly interwoven into the fabric of the society? Finally, we must note Duhl's concluding remarks that the psychiatrist "must play a role in *controlling* the environment which man has created." At the risk of being facetious, I might point out that apparently the American psychiatrist is being asked to usurp the role of the political parties on the radical left. In sum, these and numerous other papers and remarks support my contention that it is the rational model of the social system that is providing the theoretical underpinnings for community psychiatry.

REALITIES ABOUT MENTAL ILLNESS

If the community psychiatrist is a skilled professional utilizing his knowledge to detect, diagnose, treat and prevent mental disorders in the community both by working with individuals and in institutions, then he must take cognizance of certain known facts about mental illness. If he ignores these facts in the design of programs, there is a good probability that he will be frustrated with the results of community psychiatric practices:

The relevant facts about mental illness include the following:

(1) Evidence has been increasing that the psychoses of the central age groups have not increased in the United States over the past two or three generations.[7]

(2) There is mounting evidence that the major mental disease, schizophrenia, is found in

every culture of the world and at every social level in those cultures.[8]

(3) The manic-depressive psychoses have, for the most part, been eliminated from hospitals and are being managed in the community due to the increase of office psychiatric practice.[9]

(4) There is some fairly reliable evidence for the possibility that some kind of genetic defect is operative in the etiology of selected psychoses, certain types of mental deficiency and certain psychophysiological disorders.[10]

(5) Epidemiological evidence shows that the psychopathic, situational and personality disturbances are highly concentrated in the culturally and economically impoverished areas of our communities.[11]

(6) The reinforcing aspect of certain types of environment for various kinds of mental symptoms is a fact that is clearly recognized.[12]

(7) Mounting evidence indicates that the various psychotherapeutic techniques are extremely uncertain with respect to outcome.[13]

(8) The detection and treatment of childhood schizophrenia has not prevented this disorder from occurring when these children have become adults.[14]

It appears that community psychiatry is an attempt to develop a new role and function for the psychiatrist. But in so doing, it often seems to ignore these realities about mental health and illness. These realities are stubborn ones and it is difficult to see how the new theory and techniques with which the community psychiatrist is to be equipped will eliminate or change these facts.

Therefore, in all likelihood, the big opportunity for a community psychiatry will come through the increase of various kinds of nonconforming behavior accompanied by a corresponding decrease in tolerance for nonconformity. These both may be consequences of forces operating in contemporary middle-class, urbanized, bureaucratic society. Such a situation has been foreshadowed in numerous ways by Duhl, and it is now a standard contention in community psychiatry that the reduction of these kinds of deviancy can be obtained by the strengthening of our basic social institutions: family, school and church. But, of course, herein lies a great dilemma: How do we do this without enhancing and reinforcing those institutional social values which have proved so unrealistic for contemporary society?

The increase in social judgments regarding nonconforming behavior can be diagramed by showing the relationships between clinical and societal judgments as to who is to be defined as mentally ill (Figure 6.1). There are, of course, four possibilities here.[15] (A) A person can be defined as mentally ill by his significant others, acting as society's representatives, and also can be judged mentally ill on clinical examination. (B) He can be defined as mentally ill by his significant others but not mentally ill on clinical examination. (C) He can be defined by his significant

Figure 6.1. Model of Relationship Between
Societal and Clinical Judgments
of Mental Illness

Societal Judgment	Clinical Judgment	
	Mentally ill	Not Mentally ill
Mentally ill	(A) Psychotics	(B) Character Disturbances
Not Mentally ill	(C) Psychoneurotics	(D) Normals

others as not mentally ill but judged mentally ill on clinical examination. (D) He can be defined as not mentally ill by his significant others and not mentally ill on clinical examination. In cell A, where the two judgments coincide on mental illness, all psychotics should be found; in cell B, behavioral and character disturbances; in cell C, psychoneurotics; and in cell D, so-called normals. Our primary concern is with cells B and C, for this is where societal and clinical judgments are moving closer together as a reflection of the continuing and growing pressure to eliminate all types of nonconformity from our increasingly middle-class society.

The fact that the social and clinical judgments represented in cells B and C are very loose is supported by the great variations in rates on nonconforming behavior which have been reported in epidemiological studies conducted in different parts of the world. For example, on examining these studies, I have found marked variation in total rates reported from surveys of all psychiatric disorders. However, these variations are reduced considerably when only rates for total psychoses are considered. The variations in rates between different cultures and nations are further reduced when only the rates for schizophrenia are considered.[16] The findings from these studies point clearly to the fact that the difficulty lies in the fluctuations of social and clinical judgments in cells B and C.

I have discussed in various contexts what I have termed the widening definition of mental illness. It is the growing number of cases which fall in cells B and C which reflect this expansiveness of judgments about mental illness. Symptom criteria, both socially and clinically, for who is to be selected for these two cells will continue to be distorted by social values and preferences.[17]

Given the difficulties implicit in arriving at valid clinical judgments, it almost staggers the imagination to see how the community psychiatrist will operate when faced in various institutions with numerous persons and cliques presently regarded to fall within a normal range. As I interpret it, the community psychiatrist is to play a role in restructuring organizations so that they function more harmoniously and in providing environments for persons that will facilitate more healthy development and behavior. His goal here is to increase societal competence in carrying out the socialization process toward the end of obtaining mentally healthy personalities. This creates a range of implications and problems which the community psychiatrist must face.

THE POLITICS OF COMMUNITY PSYCHIATRY

First, the community psychiatrist faces the problem of how to get involved in an organization while maintaining enough distance and detachment to view the operation objectively and advise accordingly. Here he encounters an acute methodological difficulty often apparent in sociological and anthropological research. The anthropologist, in his studies of various cultures, attempts to solve the involvement-detachment problem by going into a given culture for a short time, making observations, securing data from informants, and then immediately coming out in order to conceptualize the manner in which the culture is organized and how it functions. At this point, he is nearly always struck with the doubt that he ever got deep enough into the culture to gain real comprehension and understanding. Consequently, he sometimes chooses to make a second attempt, going into the culture for a long time, acquiring the language, adopting the customs, participating in the ceremonies and maybe even taking a native wife; now, he may have become so immersed in the new cultural world that upon his departure he finds it difficult to report exactly what he has found out about the society.

The community psychiatrist may find himself in this dilemma when he seriously attempts to become involved in an organization. He would particularly find the going rough if his involvement reaches the level of entering the political arena and competing for public office, involving himself in numerous reciprocal promises and obligations. It is noteworthy that a parallel dilemma is often faced by the clinical psychiatrists involved in various forms of psychotherapy: there is always the danger of emotional involvement with the patient with the consequent inability to unravel the various emotional strands (there have been a few cases where analysts have married their patients).

A second problem for the community psychiatrist centers around the ends that are to be achieved by working through various organizations and institutions within the community. As he becomes involved in urban renewal, community planning programs, industrial strife, poverty programs, retraining programs, family groups and university conflicts, he faces this problem most acutely: What is the correspondence between the ends toward which he is working and those toward which he wants to work? The goals of many of these programs and organizations are amorphous, general and uncertain, although typically regarded as "progressive." But in fact, the goals flow out of the collective life of the organization; as they are modified, changed and redirected, they form a gigantic mosaic of the organization as it moves through time. Many of the ends toward which communities and institutions strive are centered upon specifics such as better housing, more health facilities, improved schools, up-to-date technology, better roads, new public health facilities and increased profits. While there is little that is novel about such aspirations, conflicts typically emerge over the best means to obtain them. Equally significant is determining if sought-after goals really constitute improvements over past situations. We employ many statistical indices to measure our progress, such as changes in mortality rates, rates of mental illness, net production and the rise and fall of the price index. All of these are indications of changes that have taken place in our communities over time. How does the community psychiatrist work within these goal structures, many of which are by no means of his own making? Is he to direct his energy in the business organization toward improving the mental health levels of the personnel, increasing its total efficiency, reducing the tensions involved in interpersonal relationships, improving the morale of the organization, clarifying the relationship of the organizational conformity, increasing the payments in workmen's compensation or lowering the age of retirement? Or should he attempt to do all of these things? Will not simultaneous seeking of several of these ends constantly face him with conflict and impossible decisions?

This is not an attempt to throw obstacles in the path of the community psychiatrist: I am only trying to indicate that our knowledge and skill with respect to intervening in the life of a community, an institution or a society, particularly with reference to general goals, is extremely minimal. Involvement in such real-world situations is a far more complex business than taking over some of the theory and techniques of the social sciences in a limited residency training.

There is a final problem in this complex undertaking that faces the community psychiatrist: Whose agent is he? Does he function as an independent consultant on a fee basis, spelling out alternatives for an organization's accomplishment of certain goals, or does he function as a salaried member of the organization, accepting its goals and then determining how they can best be achieved? Does the community psychiatrist see himself as the agent for some governmental structure, advising, consulting and planning to bring about social conditions which will lead to a decline of behavioral deviancies and social dysfunctions in the community? Under such circumstances, does he regard himself as an official of a governmental unit, utilizing his skills to obtain certain kinds of social control that will favor the interests of certain personalities and groups?

When and if the psychiatrist leaves the clinic, hospital or private office and enters the community, he will indeed find himself in a world he never made, the land of psychiatric limbo. If he proceeds cautiously and sympathetically he will be tolerated by his new colleagues, but his anxieties and frustrations will mount with respect to the three problems discussed above. If, on the other hand, he proceeds authoritatively and with conviction, rolling out the answers with a quick and confident tongue, he will be regarded as a threat by some, as a fanatic by others.

To summarize, community psychiatry must directly face the issue of whether it possesses adequate knowledge of organization functioning for intervention to have significant consequences. Likewise, in efforts where they take roles in controlling the sociocultural environment, community psychiatrists must not only have goals clearly in mind but also face the issue whether the changes that result from intervention will actually lead to more harmonious development of individual personalities. Will controls inaugurated by a community psychiatrist constitute an improvement over the existing controls operating in our democratic society? Finally, when the psychiatrist moves from his traditional role as agent of the patient or hospital and becomes the agent of some larger community-based organization, either public or private, how will he be able to retain his true identity and function? Is it not likely that he will find himself serving ends that he only dimly comprehends? Might he not move in the direction of controls that will serve the purposes of certain persons and groups to the disadvantage of other persons and groups?

I have intentionally been critical in order to highlight these issues as sharply as possible. Large sums of money have been, are and probably will continue to be available to cope as adequately as we possibly can with mental illness and to bring about those social and economic conditions that will enhance mental health. Numerous questions, issues and dilemmas must be faced forthrightly if we are ever to spend the available monies in a manner to achieve the highest possible level of welfare and mental health for our people.

REFERENCES

1. See Chapter 5.
2. Leonard J. Duhl, "The Psychiatric Evolution," in *Concepts of Community Psychiatry: A Framework for Training* (U.S. Department of Health, Education and Welfare), pp. 19–32; "The Psychiatrist in Urban Social Planning," paper presented at colloquium, Brandeis University, Florence Heller Graduate School for Advanced Studies in Social Welfare (March 11, 1965), mimeographed; "New Directions in Mental Health Planning," *Archives of General Psychiatry*, 13 (November 1965): 403–410; and "Mental Health and the Urban World," paper presented at the White House Conference on Health, Washington, D.C. (November 3–4, 1965), mimeographed.
3. *Education for Community Psychiatry*, G.A.P. Circular Letter No. 344.
4. Karl R. Popper, *The Open Society and Its Enemies*, vols. 1 and 2 (New York: Harper & Row, 1963), and *Poverty of Historicism* (New York: Harper & Row, 1964).
5. *Op. cit.*, GAP Report.
6. Leonard J. Duhl, "The Changing Face of Mental Health," paper presented at the Detroit Re-

gional Meeting of the American Psychiatric Association (October 29–31, 1959) (reprinted by the Department of Health, Education and Welfare), pp. 60–74.

7. H. Goldhamer and A. Marshall, *Psychosis and Civilization* (Glencoe, Illinois: The Free Press, 1953). See also H. Warren Dunham, *Sociological Theory and Mental Disorder*, chap. 6 (Detroit: Wayne State University Press, 1959).

8. N. J. Demerath, "Schizophrenia Among Primitives," *American Journal of Psychiatry*, 98 (1942): 703. See also P. K. Benedict and I. Jacks, "Mental Illness in Primitive Societies," *Psychiatry*, 17 (1954): 377; E. F. B. Forster: "Schizophrenia as Seen in Ghana," *Congress Report of the Second International Congress for Psychiatry*, 1 (1959): 151; P. M. Yap: "A Diagnostic and Prognostic Study of Schizophrenia in Southern Chinese," *Congress Report of the Second International Congress for Psychiatry*, 1 (1959): 354; and T. Lin, "A Study of the Incidence of Mental Disorder in Chinese and Other Cultures," *Psychiatry*, 16 (1953): 313.

9. H. Warren Dunham, *Community and Schizophrenia: An Epidemiological Analysis* (Detroit: Michigan: Wayne State University Press, 1965), table 90.

10. J. Böök, "A Genetic and Neuropsychiatric Investigation of a North Swedish Population," *Acta Genetica et Statistica Medica*, 4 (1958): 1–100. See also F. J. Kallman, "The Genetic Theory of Schizophrenia," *American Journal of Psy-*

chiatry, 103 (1946): 309; *Heredity in Health and Mental Disorder* (New York: Norton, 1953).

11. A. Leighton, *et al., The Character of Danger* (New York: Basic Books, 1963). See also H. Warren Dunham, *Community and Schizophrenia: An Epidemiological Analysis* (Detroit: Wayne State University Press, 1965), chap. 9.

12. A. Leighton, *et al., ibid;* H. Warren Dunham, *ibid.* See also H. Warren Dunham and Kirson Weinberg, *The Culture of the State Mental Hospital* (Detroit: Wayne State University Press, 1960), and A. H. Stanton and M. S. Schwartz: *The Mental Hospital: A Study of Institutional Participation in Psychiatric Illness and Treatment* (New York: Basic Books, 1954).

13. Hans J. Eysenck, "The Effects of Psychotherapy," *International Journal of Psychiatry,* 1 (1) (1965): 99–144.

14. Lauretta Bender, "The Origin and Evolution of the Gestalt Function, the Body Image, and Delusional Thoughts in Schizophrenia," in *Recent Advances in Biological Psychiatry,* 5 (New York: Plenum Press, 1963), and "Schizophrenia in Childhood: Its Recognition, Description and Treatment," *American Journal of Orthopsychiatry,* 26 (1956): 499.

15. This model has been discussed in H. Warren Dunham, "Epidemiology of Psychiatric Disorders as a Contribution to Medical Ecology," *Archives of General Psychiatry,* 14 (January, 1966): 1–19.

16. Dunham, *op. cit.*

17. Tsung-yi Lin, "The Epidemiological Study of Mental Disorders," *WHO Chronicle,* 21 (12) (December, 1967): 509–516. This excellent analysis supports my contention of the increasing pressure in cells *B* and *C.*

—7—

Whither Community Psychiatry?

In this chapter my concerns are three: first, to examine the nature of community psychiatry; second, to analyze the need for a community psychiatry; and third, to explore some of the implications of community psychiatry as a new psychiatric specialty.

It must be painfully clear to anyone viewing the current mental health scene that there is great confusion as to what constitutes this new psychiatric specialty. This is certainly true for the majority of psychiatrists now practicing in this country, because they have been trained to carry out therapeutic functions completely different from those emphasized by this newly emergent psychiatric specialty. It is, of course, recognized that certain persons in the field of

Read at the World Congress of Mental Health, London, August 1968.

psychiatry have attempted to carve out what they considered to be the broad outline of this new specialty, which reads very much like a graduate curriculum for students in sociology and social psychology. However, the question still remains, If psychiatrists do receive the type of training currently recommended in various residency programs, what exactly would they do in the community to maximize the conditions for the mental health of the people who compose it? Of course, it should be made clear at this point that I do not intend, as some mental health professionals apparently do, to tie community psychiatry to the new community mental health center, an entirely different type of entity. The community mental health center represents an attempt to bring all available treatment techniques and facilities under one roof, or in one area, to serve a limited population. It does not necessarily follow, however, as certain people have assumed, that because you have a community mental health center, therefore you need a new specialty, namely, a community psychiatry. Thus, until a clearer conception of the nature of community psychiatry develops and a clearer conception as to what the community psychiatrist is going to do, it is extremely doubtful that much headway in treating and caring for the mentally ill will be made from this perspective. Even if such conceptions became crystal clear to all psychiatrists, I am most skeptical that such clarity would result even eventually in a decrease in mental ill-health for a community population. Rather, the result in all likelihood would be the utilization of psychiatry as another instrument of the state to secure an increase of the social-control mechanisms in the community.

To speak of the need for community psychiatry implies, of course, that we know what community psychiatry is. This is, as we have just shown in the light of competing conceptions, an almost impossible task. Great confusion exists among psychiatrists themselves as to what body of knowledge and skills should be in the possession of a community psychiatrist. However, the notion of the need for community psychiatrists has, in my judgment, been unwittingly prepared by a host of social scientists who like to view the society as pathological rather than the person.

During the past 30 years we have been subjected to literally an avalanche of books purporting to deal with society or the community as a patient in contrast to the person. Such titles as *The Sick Society*[1], *The Neurotic Personality of Our Time*[2], *Society as the Patient*[3], *The Juvenile in Delinquent Society*[4], and *Community as Doctor*[5], are only some examples of social science studies that have provided a scientific base for the development of a community psychiatry. Now, my reference to these works in this context does not imply that they had no significant points to make on their own. Indeed they did, and they called attention to the fact that there were aspects of current social structures that might be corrected and changed in the interest of the welfare of the people who compose them. These books might be said to present selected theoretical models of society rather than to serve as a directive for social action to secure certain desired ends. However, I think that these books have had, along with selected Freudian thought, an impact upon the psychiatric community and have created a notion that much more can be done to treat and to prevent the development of mental illness than has been done in the past.

However, I think that there is also another pressure that has led to this emphasis on the need for community psychiatry. Here, I am referring to what I have called elsewhere the widening definition of mental illness.[6] By this I mean that as a society we have become more narrow and intolerant of the varieties of behavior that in the past were tolerated and accepted by people at the several class levels of the society. This is the pressure for conformity which increases sharply with the emergence of the bureaucratized and computerized society. In such societies men are reduced to numbers, with the result that they lose their own individuality, and so they struggle to find new ways for identity and recognition of the self. But in such societies in our Western world, the power concentrations are so great as to provide numerous pressures for limiting the various kinds of nonconformity that might develop. It is in this attempt to limit and to narrow the range of acceptable human behavior that we get a widening definition of what constitutes mental illness.

In this sense the current hippie movement which attracts a certain percentage of our youth takes on a new character, for here one sees a group of young people who have turned their backs on the contemporary conventions of our current society and have said, "What's the use—to hell with it—we'll go our own ways—it makes no difference what we do, we are lost anyway"—or more bluntly, "Everyone's fucked up." I cannot but refer to the remarks of a well-known anthropologist of my acquaintance whom I ran into at a recent convention in San Francisco just after he had visited the hippie kingdom in the Haight-Ashbury district. He turned to me and said, "They're sick, they're all sick, that is all that is the matter and it is terrible what they are doing to themselves." The latter observation may be justified in that by their behavior they are building up consequences for themselves that may prove most costly with the passage of time. But the point that I am concerned with is the widening definition of what constitutes mental ill-health. In other words, if you don't go along with the crowd, you're likely to be labeled as mentally ill. It is this attitude to which I object, and it is this type of behavior to which some people refer when they speak of a need for a community psychiatry.

Let us turn now to some of the implications of the development of a community psychiatry. These implications, in my judgment, are three in number but, in general, lack the essential evidence to support them. The three implications to which I refer are: (1) the notion concerning the nature of community, (2) the notion of the community as a causative agent and (3) the notion that there is some form of community organization conducive to mental health.

Let us examine each one of these implications in more detail. The notion of a community is extremely old and can indeed be traced back to classical times. Many writers and analysts have attempted to describe and to delimit the nature of a community, and to define community boundaries. And while many notions have developed and many conceptions of community have been accepted at different times, nevertheless, there is in some of these conceptions the implication that the community can be acted upon in a fashion somewhat similar to that of acting upon the individual. This patently is not true—it is absurd—but this view has emerged because of the overwhelming power that social influences and forces had in shaping the intellectual development of certain persons.

Perhaps one of the most extreme conceptions concerning the community has been expressed by the Austrian-Polish sociologist Ludwig Gumplowicz (1838–1909).[7] In a statement about the nature of sociology Gumplowicz produced a famous aphorism, namely, "It is not the individual that thinks, but it is the community that thinks." Now it must be perfectly clear that a community does not think in the same fashion as does a person. A community through its individual members can arrive at a decision to formulate a policy, can agree on some consensus and can develop ideas and points of view in a discussion that were not present in the minds of any of the members that compose the community before discussion began. However, this process is different in nature from the thought process as it occurs in the person. Now, I emphasize this extreme viewpoint about the nature of community because it highlights a dilemma faced by the new community psychiatrist. If the psychiatrist employs those techniques he has acquired for working with—that is, treating—the community, will he have any impact on the individual who is mentally ill? What is the entity that he is attempting to treat? Are there any techniques, any procedures or any patterns of authority that can be established as useful in dealing with the community so that it will maximize the conditions for mental health for the people that compose it? At this point, as far as I know, no such tested procedures are available.

A second implication of this new psychiatric specialty, community psychiatry, is the notion that the community through its collection of families, its organizational character and its general pathological and disorganized aspects, is in some way responsible for any mental illness that may develop among the people who constitute it.

Now, of course, this position raises a host of problems for which satisfactory answers are not easily forthcoming. There are certain forms of behavior, certain adult character disorders, certain patterns of nonconformity, certain symptomatic patterns that we label as psychoneuroses that may well indeed have their roots in the character of our social life. But even here, the cause of these links is by no means conclusively established. We have numerous hypotheses, we have various perspectives and we have a certain amount of evidence attempting to link these psychological disturbances with the conditions of social organization. But there are many gaps in our knowledge here. These gaps will be particularly noticeable if we attempt to develop therapeutic procedures oriented with respect to the community that are supposed to cope with these mental ill-health conditions that have developed and are developing among certain persons in the community.

There is no doubt that such an entity as social causation operates. But we should be very clear and very specific as to how far we will permit ourselves to go in showing that certain types of abnormal behavior which we see in persons are socially induced. If we are not clear concerning the social causative path and if we do not act from a body of established knowledge, we only raise doubt among the people as to the validity of the procedures that we attempt to utilize in treating the community.

There is one final implication of community psychiatry that needs to be emphasized. This is the notion that there is some form of social organization that will maximize the conditions promoting mental health, in contrast to other types of social organization which will maximize the conditions promoting mental ill-health among the people of the community. When one moves about and observes carefully the various types of cultural organization that are found in different parts of the world, one faces a very difficult problem in attempting to determine whether one type of cultural organization is more conducive to mental health than another. Any attempt to arrive at some decision is obviously handicapped by the lack of adequate statistical comparison between countries and cultures. For these figures that would provide confidence for us do not really exist, and we have no means of determining that one cultural organization is more conducive to mental health than another. Actually, what seems to be happening in the highly technically organized societies in the world is the tendency, as I pointed out previously, to check all nonconformity and to find ways and means for eliminating such nonconformity from the community.

This implication provides such a large topic that it is difficult to know what to include. It has been clear for some time that as far as the major psychoses are concerned, psychoses at least as we understand them in the Western world are distributed as a worldwide phenomenon. With respect to the minor types of mental disturbances as represented by psychopathies, character disorders and psychoneuroses, the exact variations, as I have indicated, from culture to culture are actually unknown. Thus, we have no basis for determining that one kind of cultural organization will be more conducive to mental health than another.

These implications pose a perplexing problem for the community psychiatrist. Where is he going to intervene in a culture; where is he going to cut into a community that will enable him to maximize the conditions promoting the mental health of the people? This is the situation which he faces and, with no guidelines available, it seems at least premature to attempt to develop this new psychiatric specialty when in the final analysis we have been so unsuccessful in therapeutic results for the major types of mental disturbances.

Thus, in this chapter I have attempted to examine the nature of this new specialty called community psychiatry, the need for a community psychiatry and particularly its implications. Until we have clearer answers with respect to these implications, it seems a most uncertain procedure, and a rather dangerous one, to turn our psychiatric energies to the treatment of community organization as a means for supposedly arresting mental illness when we know so little about treatment techniques on the community level and how they work.

I am well aware of the pessimistic note that I am striking in these remarks and, of course, I have no intention of striking it. Rather, my aim is to direct our energies, our resources and our research techniques towards those areas where we have a chance of coming up with significant answers that may help us in the future.

REFERENCES

1. Arthur James Israel Kraus, *The Sick Society* (Chicago: University of Chicago Press, 1929), pp. x–206. This English edition, revised by the University of Chicago Press, is a translation, in part, of the author's original German manuscripts *Die kranke Gesellschaft* and *Die menschliche Leistungsfahigkeit.* The English and German editions

contain the philosophical trend of thought which is omitted in the present revised issue.

2. Karen Horney, *The Neurotic Personality of Our Time* (New York: Norton, 1937), pp. xii, 13–299.
3. Lawrence Frank, *Society As the Patient: Essays on Culture and Personality* (New Brunswick: Rutgers University Press, 1948), pp. xiv, 395.
4. Milton Barron, *The Juvenile in Delinquent Society* (New York: Knopf, 1954), p. 349.
5. Robert N. Rapoport with the collaboration of Rhona Rapoport and Irving Rosow. *Community As Doctor: New Perspectives on a Therapeutic Community*, (London: Tavistock publications; Springfield, Illinois: C. C. Thomas, 1960), p. 325.
6. See my discussion in Chapter 5.
7. Ludwig Gumplowicz, *Outlines of Sociology*, 2d English language edition (New York: Payne and Whitman, 1963), edited and introduction by I. Horowitz.

—8—

Early Hospital Release of Schizophrenic Patients: Some Consequences to Family and Community

In this chapter I intend to examine the current policy concerning the early hospital discharge of schizophrenic patients. First, I want to provide some kind of theoretical framework for viewing the problem. Secondly, I want to call attention to certain studies that have helped to illuminate facets of this problem and to clarify our thinking with respect to those factors that should be discussed in any critical analysis.

As a prelude to this analysis it might be very much to the point to examine the motives that argue

Presented before New York Psychiatric Society, February 10, 1972; also before a session of the Annual Meeting of the American Psychiatric Association, Dallas, Texas, May 2, 1972.

for and support the efforts to return the hospitalized schizophrenic to his family and community as quickly as possible. Three such motives have been clearly identified. First, there is the economic motive. This motive is based on certain evidence which demonstrates that it is economically advantageous for the taxpayer to maintain a schizophrenic in the community rather than in the hospital. Second, there is the humanitarian motive. This motive stems from a compassion and sympathy for the patient's condition. Here, the mental hospital is viewed as a formal, bureaucratic, confining and impersonal institution. In contrast, the family is informal, loosely structured, freedom-giving and personal. The patient will naturally thrive better in the latter situation. Third, there is the cultural motive. This motive is found in a belief that stresses the sacredness of the family. This belief emphasizes the values of integration, unity, sharing and togetherness with the family. As such, both the patient and family are served by reuniting the patient with his family as soon as the patient's condition permits. In the light of these motives it is interesting to note that there are no scientific findings to support the notion that the schizophrenic patient will improve more quickly in the family setting or that the family will be strengthened by receiving the patient after a brief hospitalization. In fact, that psychiatric theory that portrays the genesis of the disorder as embedded in the psychodynamics of the family, encourages a skepticism of efforts to return the patient to his family, especially his family of orientation.

Any consideration of the impact of short or long

hospitalization of schizophrenics on their families and communities must be analyzed in terms of the diverse types of families and communities that are found in society today as well as the social changes that seemingly are sweeping through all social institutions of the Western world. A superficial examination of the topic seems to imply that the patterns of hospitalization of schizophrenics have been changing by reducing the length of hospitalization, by the utilization of drugs to control the patient on the outside, by the development of crisis psychiatric intervention, by the establishment of day and night hospitals, by the continuity of care provided by the new community mental health centers and by the use of psychiatric consultations to community institutions. Further, the implication seems to be that the family and the community as constituting the organizational arrangements external to the patients have remained relatively unchanged, merely waiting to experience the absorption of those schizophrenic patients who formerly were absorbed by the mental hospital, quite often for a lifetime.

Of course, such a picture is completely unwarranted. While there is no doubt that patterns of hospitalization with respect to schizophrenic patients have changed tremendously, it is also true that the same period, roughly the quarter of a century following World War II, reflected significant changes in both the family and the community—changes that were not predictable by the social scientist during the period under examination. Without even attempting to assess all the changes that have occurred in the contemporary family, it seems useful for our purpose to point to a few highly visible ones.

In this period the suburban family has come into existence, leaving large urban communities to the blacks and the economically less successful whites. This pattern is particularly noticeable in the cities across the north and central part of the nation from Boston to St. Louis. When I say that the suburban family has come into existence, I am not referring to the upper-class and upper-middle-class family which sought the suburban atmosphere many years ago. Rather, I am referring to the suburban family that cuts across all social class lines from the manual workers to the professionals, all escapees from the decay of our cities.[1]

Swanson and Miller[2] attempt to assess another change in the family when they describe the emergence of the bureaucratic family in contrast to the entrepreneurial family. It is, of course, the former that has been increasing in numbers. The bureaucratic family is characterized mainly by the employment of the father in one of our large institutions such as a business corporation, a university, a hospital, a school system, a military organization or a governmental structure. He works for a yearly salary, his work is appraised and supervised and he is in some hierarchal arrangement that will be governed by some plan of selection and promotion for some still-higher-paid work. Again the bureaucratic family cuts across all class lines ranging from the policeman or skilled mechanic to the highest-paid corporation president.

Seeley and others[3] in their study of one suburban community in Canada have described in an interesting fashion a conflict of parental values in child training. The father tends to emphasize initiative, courage and independence while the mother emphasizes group acceptance, belonging and popularity among peers. To be accepted, to have a role, to be recognized is much more important than to challenge the group by taking an unpopular stand even though it may be something in which the person deeply believes.

A fourth characteristic of the contemporary suburban family is the marked weakening of kinship ties, a process that was in evidence before World War II but that is continuing to accelerate as both residential and vertical mobility of families have increased.[4] The men of upwardly mobile families have in fact been frequently advised by their corporate managers that they face the necessity of breaking ties with old friends and even family members as they move upward in the corporate structure.[5] This tends to make social relationships very fragmented, unreal and ephemeral and produces what Reisman[6] has called the "lonely crowd" of American society. One can imagine that in such a family a schizophrenic would be a real problem, and if the family is economically secure enough, it is likely to be solved by hospitalizing the person in one of our most expensive hospitals.

With the rise of the suburban family that cuts across all class lines, the characteristics of the community as it has been pictured in the past have, for all practical purposes, disappeared. The urban community, especially the older neighborhood, has often been devastated. The exodus of urban families has been brought about by urban renewal programs, the relocation of manufacturing and service industries in the suburbs, the deterioration of the urban schools and the increasing physical and vocal demands of our black citizens for a larger share in the affluent society. This weakening of the urban neighborhood because of the exodus of many of its leaders has tended to weaken the economic power that is useful in getting things done. It has also produced a certain malaise characterized by confusion, uncertainty and cynicism among those persons still remaining in the city.

The new communities that have emerged on the periphery of the decaying cities have an artificial character. Here, of course, life styles and social patterns are varied, and perhaps no one characteristic can be pointed to as typical. It seems, however, that people living in them have social contacts more than friends, that competition for high social standing is the order of the day and, finally, that most of them seem to be characterized by a denial pattern: that is, the people in them want to close their eyes to the various social pathologies such as crime, delinquency, drug usage, mental illness and racial conflict. They are always present somewhere else, but not in "our" community. For example, drug usage was no problem until it hit the middle-class suburbs; then it became a "real" problem and all the resources of the middle-class community were called upon to combat it.

Here I have attempted in a few short paragraphs to characterize the situation in contemporary families and communities as they have been literally ravaged by the winds of change. New York City might be described as an ageing whore who still has a lot to give, but takes plenty in return. Thus, the entire picture of the contemporary family and community is part of a vast change that is taking place in all of our social institutions as they strive for new images, rationalizations, structures and policies geared to people's needs.

Consequently, the impact of short hospitalization of the schizophrenic on the family cannot be analyzed in a simple fashion. The problem is complex not only because of the swiftness of social change, but also because of the existence of the diverse types of families and communities.

Two basic questions must be raised and confronted: (1) What are the advantages and disadvantages to the patient of returning him to his family and community after a brief hospitalization? (2) What are the advantages and disadvantages to the family and community of receiving the returned patient after a brief hospitalization? When one confronts these two questions, one can immediately sense the complexity of the problem. Among some mental health workers there is frequently the unspoken assumption that getting the schizophrenic patient back to his family as soon as possible will not only benefit the patient, but in some unexplained way contribute to the unity and integration of the family.

The isolation of the social-breakdown syndrome as reported by Gruenberg,[7] along with suggestions for its prevention, represents a possibility for enabling patients, particularly schizophrenics, to reenter the community rather quickly. As Gruenberg states, the social-breakdown syndrome emerges when the person is unable to comply with the demands placed upon him by others in his environment. Thus, if the demands were to be decreased, it might be possible to prevent the more obvious manifestations of this syndrome. However, it should be noted that if this syndrome is valid and can be prevented, it would help to ease the burden on family members of coping with both the released patient and the patient who may never need to be hospitalized.

Again, the problem is complex because the advantages and disadvantages to the patient and to his family are very much likely to revolve around whether the patient returns to the family of orientation or the family of procreation. In addition, the nature of the relationship between these two families, if they live in the same community, may be crucial for keeping the patient in the family once he has returned. However, regardless of this additional complexity, the patient is supposedly benefited by an arresting of a possible chronicity, an early disruption of his adaptation to hospital life, an occasion to utilize techniques of rehabilitation, the opportunity to assume certain social roles he had before he was sick and, in general, surrounding him with persons who are concerned for his welfare. All of these things, of course, are regarded as positive advantages, but one has to point out that the extent to which they emerge as advantages will be dependent upon the type of family that receives the patient. As a general rule, one might assert that the more integrated and economically secure the family is, the better it will be able to absorb the shock of mental hospitalization for one of its members. As a corollary to this proposition, it can also be asserted that the shock of mental hospitalization of a family member can be absorbed more easily if that member has a minor role in contrast to a major role in the family.

This proposition has already been carefully documented in the work of Freeman and Simmons,[8] where they state that the continued community care of former patients (in their sample, the great majority were schizophrenics) is primarily dependent upon the character of the family settings and the interpersonal relationships within the family. They also emphasize that if a patient has no contact with professional persons in the community, he has a greater probability of staying in the community and not returning to the hospital.

We gain additional perspective on this issue by considering some of the recent models of mental illness that have been discussed. Ederyn Williams[9] in an interesting article analyzes the various models that have been proposed. She considers the traditional medical model which sees the institution as a mental hospital and contrasts this model with behavioral, imprisonment and hedonic models. The imprisonment model she attributes to the writings of Goffman[10] and Laing,[11] where the institution becomes a prison and the patients become prisoners. In the hedonic model described by the Braginskys,[12] the institution is regarded as a resort and the inmates are holidaymakers or refugees. In this latter model the emphasis is on the use of the hospital as an escape and as a refuge from the sordid aspects of community and family life. The person literally comes to the hospital to rest and forget the pressures to which he has been subjected in his family and in his community. It is perhaps more than interesting that such a model emerges at a time when the family is attempting to cope with tremendous strains and when the more traditional community is breaking up or is literally disappearing with the advent of the planned and artificial community as opposed to the natural community.

Now I hold no particular brief for any of these models. In my judgment, the error in all of them is that of trying to use any one of the models as a total explanation for mental patients in mental hospitals. Rather, it would be closer to the truth to state that one can find some patients in every mental hospital who would certainly fit each one of the suggested models. This comment is supported by noting the variation in the etiological agent associated with each model. In the medical model, cause is due to infection or genetic defect; in the behavioristic model, to mal-learning; in the imprisonment model, to a deviant sub-culture;* and in the hedonic model; to social

*It should be noted here that Williams views the etiology for this model as "unclear." I have attributed "cause" to a deviant subculture.

poverty. Again, the groups that supposedly prefer these models are psychiatrists, psychologists, sociologists and inmates respectively.

This analysis by Williams is one of many examples in the psychiatric field in which one is made acutely aware of the close tie-up of theoretical positions with the social and cultural conditions prevailing at a given period. That is, eventually some seminal mind is going to appear which will see the connection and write a brilliant treatise on this relationship, pointing to the instability of the various psychiatric theories, the tendency for certain repetitions to appear among them over a period of time and their ties with certain attitudinal and ideological factors that are present at a given time in history. When such an analysis is completed from a general perspective of the sociology of knowledge, it will probably then be possible to sort out the causative conditions related to given kinds of cases rather than to expend effort in coping with mental illness as a generic entity.

In this analysis, up to the present, I have attempted to indicate the variability of family patterns and community organizations that emerges as a consequence of the swift and flagrant social changes that have been sweeping all of our institutions. As indicated above, one can hardly comment on the impact of the early release of schizophrenic patients upon the family and the community but can only comment on such impact in relationship to the various types of families and communities. However, one can refer to certain general influences which have been documented in the literature and which will produce different ways of coping with them in the various types of families and communities. I state these consequences in propositional form:

(1) The shortening of the stay of schizophrenic patients in the hospitals, and their return to the family and the community, has produced an increase in the marital and reproductive rates of schizophrenic patients. This proposition has been documented for a 20-year period in New York State through the work of Erlenmeyer-Kimling[13] and her colleagues in the New York State Psychiatric Institute.

(2) The use of drugs has increased significantly for the purpose of managing prematurely released schizophrenic patients and also schizophrenic outpatients who reject hospitalization. This increased use of drugs means that the family has to be cooperative in getting the patient to take the drugs.[14]

(3) The presence of a schizophrenic patient in the family means that extra effort must be expended by each family member in supporting and caring for the schizophrenic patient. This is particularly true when one notes that the returned schizophrenic patient is unable to effectively carry out his previous role or roles in the family setting.[15] Certain investigators[16] have pointed out that the association between community tolerance and performance is supported by the fact that patients with the most bizarre and acute symptoms are returned to the hospital sooner.

(4) With the presence in the family of a schizophrenic patient, the family members constantly carry the psychological burden of explaining the sick

person's behavior and verbal expressions to friends and others. This may mean that the family, in order to maintain its own sense of unity and integration, may tend to withdraw from intense social contacts with friends and neighbors. Freeman,[17] in a thoughtful comment on community mental health, warns of some of the pitfalls of passing the burden of the mental patient on to the family. The social price of maintaining unrecovered schizophrenics and certain inadequate personalities in their families and communities, may be in the long run more costly than any monies saved by a reduction of the period of hospitalization.

(5) The return of the hospitalized schizophrenic becomes a financial burden if he is unable to assume his former economic responsibilities. This problem, of course, is more acute with a family on a low income level than it would be in a family of an upper-middle income level.

In this account I have attempted to construct a sociological framework for viewing the problem presented by the return of the schizophrenic patient to his family and community. I have pointed out that this problem can only be examined against the background of knowledge of the different types of families and communities that currently make up our social structure, for they are the social products of the swift and compelling changes of the past quarter of a century. I have tried to indicate here that the big shift that has taken place in the community is the shift from the natural to the planned or the contracted type of community, while the big shift that has taken place in the family is in terms of its economic base from the independent self-employed entrepreneur to the breadwinner who is now employed by one of our large bureaucratic organizations.

What we are seeing today of the mental patient returned to his family is perhaps nothing more than an experiment, since eventually another new and protective type of environment for the schizophrenic may be invented. I think that this will take place, but only on the condition that no final or lasting cure is discovered in the immediate future for schizophrenia.

REFERENCES

1. See, for example, A. C. Spectorsky, *The Exurbanites* (New York: George W. Steward Publisher, 1958), and Herbert Gans, *The Levittowners* (New York: Pantheon Books, 1967).
2. Guy E. Swanson and Daniel R. Miller, *The Changing American Parent: A Study in the Detroit Area* (New York: Wiley, 1958).
3. J. Seeley, R. Sims and E. W. Loosley, *Crestwood Heights* (New York: Basic Books, 1956).
4. Helen Codere, "Genealogical Study of Kinship in the United States," *Psychiatry,* 18 (1955): 65–79.
5. W. L. Warner and J. Abegglen, *Big Business Leaders in America* (New York: Athenium, 1963).

6. David Riesman, *The Lonely Crowd* (New Haven, Connecticut: Yale University Press, 1950).
7. Ernest M. Gruenberg, "Specifying the Burden on the Community: Appraising Community Care," Preprint, Psychiatric Epidemiology Research Unit, Department of Psychiatry, Columbia University, College of Physicians and Surgeons, New York, New York.
8. H. E. Freeman and O. G. Simmons, "Treatment Experiences of Mental Patients and Their Families," *American Journal of Public Health*, 51 (9) (September 1961): 1266–1273.
9. E. Williams, "Models of Madness," *New Society*, (September 30, 1971): 607–609.
10. E. Goffman, *Asylums* (Garden City, New York: Doubleday and Co., Inc. 1961).
11. R. D. Laing, *The Divided Self: An Existential in Sanity and Madness* (New York: Pantheon Books, 1960); *The Politics of Experience* (New York: Pantheon Books, 1967).
12. B. M. Braginsky, D. D. Braginsky and K. Ring, *Methods of Madness: The Mental Hospital as a Last Resort* (New York: Holt, Rinehart & Winston, 1969).
13. L. Erlenmeyer-Kimling, Susan Nicol, J. D. Rainer and W. Edwards Deming, "Changes in Fertility Rates of Schizophrenic Patients in New York State," *American Journal of Psychiatry*, 125 (January 1969): 916–927.
14. Paul Lowinger and Jacques Gottlieb, "Drug Treatment of Schizophrenic Out-Patients," *The Out-Patient Treatment of Schizophrenia* (New York: Grune & Stratton, 1960). 129–134.

15. H. E. Freeman and O. Simmons, "The Social Integration of Former Mental Patients," *International Journal of Social Psychiatry,* 4 (Spring 1959): 264–271.
16. S. Angrist, M. Lefton, S. Dinitz and B. Pasamanick, "Tolerance of Deviant Behavior, Posthospital Performance Levels and Rehospitalization," *Proceedings of the Third World Congress of Psychiatry,* 1 (Montreal, Canada: McGill University and University of Toronto Presses, 1961): 237–241.
17. H. Freeman, "Community Mental Health Action in Great Britain," *Proceedings of the Third World Congress of Psychiatry,* 1 (Montreal, Canada: McGill University and University of Toronto Presses, 1961): 292–295.

—9—

Social Action, Social Knowledge and Social Policy

The general position taken in this chapter is that our various efforts and programs to secure social action for mental health tend to outrun the knowledge and theory that we have in this area. The current cultural climate that stresses action for mental health is reflected in the bombardment of the public using such vehicles as television, radio, slick magazines and popular literature to present cases of various psychiatric conditions from which persons suffer. At the same time the case stories are used to illustrate various unproven etiological theories of mental disorder. This climate has been encouraged and supported by numerous psychiatric efforts following World War II as reflected in such works as those by Thompson[1] and Menninger.[2] These men, taking their cue from psy-

177

chiatric experience gained in World War II and noting the frequency of psychiatric problems among men inducted into the armed services, began to anticipate in their writings following the war a more positive and frontal attack on mental health problems in American society. The work of these men set the stage for the passage of the National Mental Health Act in 1948 as well as the more recent report of the Joint Commission on Mental Illness and Health in 1961. This latter report culminated in the Surgeon General's recommendation in January 1962 that the states explore a more complete utilization of all community resources dealing with the mentally ill toward achieving maximum prevention and treatment of such illnesses. Now, it seems to me in retrospect that such efforts certainly were desirable, for they have succeeded in breaking through community lethargy, outmoded state hospital cultures and lagging training and educational programs concerned with the mentally ill.

In bringing this to pass, the social scientists have also played a significant role. They have organized and analyzed the statistics of mental illness with an eye to discrepancies and contradictions; they have conducted several epidemiological studies during this period; they have explored various mental hospital cultures; they have probed and analyzed the different possibilities relative to the influence of cultural factors in the development of mental illness; and they have often served as consultants with respect to the development of numerous research, educational, treatment and rehabilitation programs for the mentally ill. These efforts of the social scientist have been both a consequence of certain initial actions and a cause for stepping up social actions with respect to mental health.

In a certain sense the entire atmosphere of the period is reflected in Jahoda's[3] careful scholarly efforts to explore the concept of positive mental health and to develop criteria that would indicate its presence or absence. In the light of the American dream it should be clear that Americans want not only to be mentally healthy but to be mentally healthy in a very positive sense, perhaps the supermen of mental health. Again, at the other end of the research spectrum,[4] as reported by a team of New York scientists, we get a gloomy picture of 80 percent of a sample of persons in midtown Manhattan as possessing selected psychiatric symptoms, a figure that is somewhat meaningless considering the fact that if the emphasis was on physical illness we would probably find 100 percent of a population had something wrong with them. On the other end of the scale these researchers report only 18 percent as severely disturbed and of this group, about four percent as incapacitated. However, the larger figure is often emphasized possibly because of its value as a propaganda device for pressuring the public for more mental health funds. This report is further troublesome because it has a double focus. On the one hand it purports to be an epidemiological study of mental disturbances in relation to age, sex, marital status and social class and on the other hand it reflects an awareness that mental disorder is one of our most pressing social problems and quick action is necessary if we are to satisfactorily cope with it.

Now, I have reviewed briefly some of the factors and developments that have served to create the current climate for social action in the mental health field. However, as I stated at the outset, perhaps a word of caution is needed now in order to recognize that our zeal to help and do something dramatic with respect to mental disorders does not outrun our available knowledge and theory, which should provide us with the assurance that we are moving in the right direction. On the face of it, it would seem that the demand to break up the large state hospitals and move toward smaller community-care hospitals, the development of day and night hospitals, convalescent homes and halfway houses as after-care units for the mentally ill, stepped-up training programs for psychiatrists and auxiliary mental health personnel, and the efforts to shorten hospital stay and get patients back into the community, if only temporarily, would seem all to the good and in the right direction. However, such developments should be fortified with a more adequate knowledge of the etiology, of the outcome and of the social consequences of mental illness in the community than we possess at the present.

Thus, let us examine several areas where our knowledge is imperfect and can produce a type of obfuscation as we proceed with our social action for mental health programs. First, let us consider the fact that in the last twenty years there has developed what I call a widening definition of mental illness. This is partially reflected in the fact that epidemiological surveys of the fifties report four to five times more mental illness than in the like studies of the twenties and thirties.[5] I think that this means not that there has been an increase in psychoses, but rather that there has been increased awareness of what we are going to label as a mental disorder and whom we are going to label as mentally disordered. This situation results in our adding to our traditional categories of mental illnesses—the psychoses, the neuroses, the psychopathies and the mental deficiencies—a fifth category of persons who are under some type of emotional and psychic stress. Such persons generally display various types of psychiatric symptoms such as anxiety, mental conflict, guilt feelings, withdrawal, compulsions, accident-proneness, nailbiting, chronic worrying and many others.

This widening definition of mental illness reflects clearly an absence of a baseline in the attempt to determine exactly who is mentally sick and who, for all practical purposes, is mentally well. For it must be remembered that in terms of psychiatric symptoms alone we are probably all mentally disturbed in much the same way as we are all physically ill. But in both instances we have illnesses that for the most part have to be ignored because we have to see that the social order functions and we have to be assured that those who care and treat the mentally ill are not as sick as the mentally ill themselves. This absence of a baseline seriously interferes with much of our research work and frequently makes it difficult to make comparative studies because different definitions of mental illness have been used.

However, this situation does not mean that psychiatric therapists should refuse to help persons who say they are sick and need help, but rather that such therapists should constantly guard against the natural professional inclination to define traits, attitudes, habits, conflicts, fears, stress and the like in persons as signs of mental illness, especially when the person himself has no such idea and further shows every indication of trying to manage his own psychological difficulties even though the method of management may not be acceptable to the therapist.

Let us consider a second issue. The Joint Commission on Mental Illness and Health, in its final report, makes a significant and interesting statement but one that is at the same time questionable. The report states, "Persons who are emotionally disturbed—that is to say, under psychological stress that they cannot tolerate—should have skilled attention and helpful counsel available to them in their community, *if the development of more serious mental breakdown is to be prevented*" (italics mine).[6] Now, there is no doubt that there would be no quarrel with this position if the authors of this report had placed a period after "community." This statement then merely represents a value position and the possibility of realizing this goal becomes largely a matter of the availability of psychiatric services and the priorities in using them. However, when the authors of the report go on to say that this is necessary if serious mental breakdown, which I am here equating with psychosis, is to be prevented, they place themselves on very questionable ground. The grounds are questionable because while clinical evidence would certainly support the position that those persons who develop severe mental disorders are under acute emotional and psychological stress, we have no very positive evidence to support the hypothesis that persons who are emotionally disturbed and under psychological stress will necessarily develop a psychosis. It seems somewhat relevant to point out in this connection that in the last fifteen years, while we have had a tremendous growth in the private practice of psychiatry, I know of no evidence to indicate that there has been a decrease in the incidence of schizophrenia in the community. On the other hand, while there may not have been an increase, it certainly does not appear that there has been a decrease. However, in a more positive vein the use of electric shock and various energizers in the treatment of depressions has greatly reduced the hospitalization of such patients.

Let us take note for a moment of the social significance of this postwar increase of the private practice of psychiatry. It has, of course, been stimulated by the easy adaptability of psychoanalysis to office practice and more recently by developments in pharmacology. But what kinds of patients are these private practicing psychiatrists treating? It is doubtful that these psychiatrists are treating the severe schizophrenics for these go eventually to the mental hospital. It is doubtful even that they are treating the severely entrenched neurotics, for their defenses are too tough to crack. It is also doubtful that they are treating the so-called psychopaths who are not likley to seek help, and if they do it is likely to be the result of law violations. It seems most likely that they are treating persons whose reality orientation is intact but who are under severe emotional and psychological stress, for which they seek help.

My recent epidemiological research[7] provided some evidence for this point. In that research I had the splendid cooperation of 82 percent of the private practicing psychiatrists in the Detroit area. On screening their records for cases in our two test subcommunities for 1956–1958 we picked up seventeen cases to whom they had given a schizophrenic diagnosis. However, we soon found that we had already picked up 76.5 percent of these cases in other facilities. We picked up at other facilities 25.4 percent of a total of 59 cases in the affective and psychoneurotic group and 21.9 percent of our 32 cases in the acting-out group. Now, these figures certainly suggest that schizophrenics who get to the private practicing psychiatrist are likely to be referred to some more appropriate facility.

Thus, it would seem that it is not completely unwarranted to infer that the private practicing psychiatrist is not treating schizophrenics—the hard core of the total mental health problem—but is rightly concentrating on those cases with whom he is likely to have a modicum of success. He is fortified in his efforts by the medical ethic which requires him to try to help those persons who say they need help.

The social significance of this situation should be clear. First, the ever-present frustration in achieving a breakthrough in dealing with the severe psychoses has caused the psychiatrist to seek—what he likes to assume are the less severe—those who are emotionally disturbed and will continue in this condition if he doesn't provide some type of therapy. These cases also permit the auxiliary professionals—social workers, psychologists and marital counselors—to make their therapeutic claims. Second, the effort expended on these cases has drained much of the brains and energy away from attention to the hardcore psychoses. Finally, these cases which our therapists rush to treat so adequately can be regarded in a sense as the failures of our culture—for their socialization in their family and peer groups have not equipped them with the personality resources to deal with the everyday problems of living with which, fortunately, the great majority of our people are equipped to cope.

Again, in another connection, the Joint Commission* goes all-out for the training of adequate personnel in depth psychotherapy, leaving short-term psychotherapy to the lesser-trained personnel, those who will utilize objective, permissive and nondirective techniques. In addition, there is the older, medically trained psychiatrist who adheres strictly to the medical model in his neurological and psychiatric

*The selection of these recommendations of the Joint Commission for critical consideration is not intended as a criticism of the total report. This is a separate task.

186 SOCIAL REALITIES AND COMMUNITY PSYCHIATRY

examinations. Thus, the Joint Commission has unwittingly established three classes of therapists in spite of the fact that our knowledge of the therapeutic benefits of long-term psychotherapy is woefully deficient, and of the kinds of cases where short-term psychotherapy may be more beneficial than long-term psychotherapy, most uncertain. In fact, the Joint Commission has placed itself in the position of advocating long-term psychotherapy while at the same time it can have no basis other than faith for knowing that it will work or with what kinds of cases it will work best. One cannot but note at this point the swing which has taken place in some psychiatric circles from an emphasis on psychological factors to an emphasis on physiological and genetic factors as being more relevant for the severe mental disorders.

It seems all too clear that our frustrations in achieving etiological breakthroughs in connection with the major psychoses, have manifested themselves in the mechanical manipulation of psychiatric services and in the development of rehabilitation programs. For it should be clear that if we had the knowledge to cure such a disorder as, for example, schizophrenia, much of our recent effort would not have been expended, and we would be less concerned with the organization of psychiatric facilities and more concerned with the techniques of getting patients well. However, this may be a continuing frustration for some years to come, and so it is only natural that mental health professionals turn to those services which will contribute to the more humane treatment of the mentally ill and make it possible for them to be fitted back in the community at certain points, even though we can hardly claim that these patients are in the best mental health. Indeed, it is possible that our best results may be along these lines in the future for much of the current etiological theory hardly holds out a promise of complete mental and personality restorations.

In these brief remarks I have tried to emphasize that good intentions are not sufficient with respect to making our plans and programs for the research, treatment and prevention of mental illness. Rather, it is necessary for us to be constantly aware of the need to direct our programs by the knowledge that we have, even though such knowledge may not always be sufficient. I have tried to call attention (1) to the inadequacies of our knowledge with respect to a baseline separating the mentally ill from the mentally well, (2) to the questionable assumption that emotional stress causes psychosis, (3) to the kinds of cases that are likely to receive treatment in the private practice of psychiatry and (4) to the unresolved issue of beneficial effects of long-term psychotherapy. It should be clear that social action with respect to mental health will only be as successful as we keep it in line with our knowledge and theory concerning the mental disorders. Thus, it is hoped that as we develop our future policies for treating and caring for our mentally ill that they will be based on scientific as well as humane foundations.[8]

REFERENCES

1. C. B. Thompson, "Psychiatry and the Social Crises," *Journal of Clinical Psychopathology,* 7 (April 1946): 697–711.
2. W. Menninger, *Psychiatry in a Troubled World* (New York: Macmillan, 1948).
3. M. Jahoda, *Current Concepts of Positive Mental Health* (New York: Basic Books, 1958).
4. L. Srole et al., *Mental Health in the Metropolis: The Mid-Town Manhattan Study* (New York: McGraw-Hill, 1962).
5. R. J. Plunkett and J. E. Gordon, *Epidemiology and Mental Illness* (New York: Basic Books, 1960).
6. Joint Commission on Mental Illness and Health, *Action for Mental Health* (New York: Basic Books, 1961), p. XII.
7. H. W. Dunham, *Community and Schizophrenia* (Detroit: Wayne State University Press, 1965).
8. See the excellent monograph by David Mechanic, *Mental Health and Social Policy* (Englewood Cliffs, New Jersey: Prentice-Hall 1969). My chapter was written before this monograph appeared.

—10—

Prospects for Community Mental Health

In the previous chapters I have been concerned primarily with a critical examination of four new psychiatric programs for the mentally ill—hospital-based therapeutic milieus, community mental health centers, community psychiatry and the early-hospital-release policy. These programs, all developed following the close of World War II, were intended to provide improved care and treatment for the mentally ill in the numerous communities across the land. These programs have come into existence as a result of the interaction of four factors: (1) large-scale government intervention in the mental health field made possible by the passage of the National Mental Health Act of 1948; (2) the growing dissatisfaction with the medical model as having utility for providing etiological hypotheses for mental disorders; (3) the several researches by both psychiatrists and sociologists depicting the structure and functions of the culture of the mental hospital; and finally (4) the general frustration experienced by practicing psychiatrists with the results of the therapies available to them in the treatment of their patients.

Now while these programs have been rationalized, in part, by various pieces of research, they gain their greatest support from certain classical values, long implicit in American society, but surfacing to a significant prominence during the past two decades. "Liberty, Equality and Fraternity," slogan of the French Revolution, epitomizes these values, always implicit in the United States Constitution but now pressing for new recognition and adequate realization in the postwar world. The value, liberty, has been emphasized by the stepped-up efforts and demands to protect the civil rights of individuals and particularly the rights of the handicapped. The drive for the achievement of greater equality is seen most clearly in the legal efforts and civil-disobedience attempts to break down those obstacles which prevent persons in minority groups from achieving their constitutionally guaranteed citizenship. And finally, the value of fraternity is reflected in the pressure to realize a wider democracy in our social institutions. During recent times such venerable institutions as the army, school, church, university, labor unions and the welfare organization have all experienced in one way or another this pressure to achieve a wider democracy. In this pressure for a more significant democracy in our several institutions traditional distinctions have been dissolved, social roles have become blurred and new "rights," have been spelled out and demanded.

The new "rights"—the right to a job, to quality health care and, of course, mental health—have been spelled out and demands have been made to the appropriate institutions. These institutions frequently are saddled with conflict, bigness, dual authority and bureaucracy and consequently are unable to deliver these new "rights." This new cultural climate with the pressure for more freedom, more equality and more democracy, in juxtaposition with the traditional medical concerns of education, research and therapy, have helped to shake our several medical institutions to their foundations. This situation has been quite noticeable in the mental health field and the programs which I have considered are, in large part, a response to what has been regarded as a failure of the traditional mental hospital, which primarily provided custodial care, sometimes good and often poor, for patients.

At this point it seems necessary to make explicit the assumptions underlying these programs. Furthermore, these assumptions, in general, are not grounded on empirical work even though now and then one can find both supporting evidence and contradictory evidence. These assumptions have been repeated so often that they are taken largely for granted. At any rate, here are the assumptions that I regard as implicit in the psychiatric programs that I have discussed.

(1) That the etiological roots of practically all mental disorders—psychoses, psychoneuroses, psychopathies and character disorders—are to be found in the social and cultural conditions that encompass the individual from birth to death. These causes include drugs, infections, traumas, environmental stress, family ties and customs.[1]

(2) That for the person who develops a mental disorder the maintenance of a close tie with his home community will be therapeutically beneficial. This has been experimented with and in part tested by those hospitals that have organized wards that receive only patients who come from a given county or township.[2]

(3) That persons who develop a mental disorder should be placed in situations which will provide a variety of continual stimuli to prevent them from becoming withdrawn and isolated.[3]

(4) That at the first sign of abnormal behavior or mentality the person should be placed in a milieu where he can receive an appropriate therapeutic intervention in order that a more serious disturbance will be prevented.[4]

(5) That the person who develops an acute mental disorder should be returned to his family as quickly as possible, for in the intimate climate provided by the family members he

will find himself in a therapeutic beneficial environment.[5]

(6) That the distinctions between the established diagnostic categories become blurred with an increased utilization of psychological and sociological forms of therapy.[6]

(7) That there are some patterns of cultural organization conducive to good mental health and other patterns of cultural organization conducive to poor mental health.

This latter assumption is more an axiom of faith[7] than a proposition resting on solid evidence. It is probably traceable to the "myth" of Rousseau's "happy savage," whose existence is unfettered by the social bonds. In the statement of this assumption there is no intent to exclude the repressive and coercive national states that by their actions create mentally unhealthy situations for thousands and millions of people living in their borders. Examples of such cases would be the persecution of the Jews in Nazi Germany in the thirties or the present practice of apartheid in South Africa. While such cases should be included, the assumption is intended to point to those more subtle forms of cultural organization that are supposedly conducive to poor mental health.

These assumptions, implicit in these programs, have been generally ignored, partially resulting from the enthusiasm that has accompanied them. Of course, as I have indicated at several points, these programs have been by no manner of means confined to the United States—in one form or another, they have been found all over the world—but, for the most part, in those areas dominated by western psychiatry. Thus, there are three additional concerns which I wish to consider briefly in the light of my analyses. They can be put in the forms of questions:

(1) Have these programs improved the patterns of care for the mentally ill in our society?

(2) Have these new programs been able to show that they have increased the number of therapeutic successes among mental patients?

(3) Have these several programs provided any indications of the direction that the care and therapy of the mentally ill will take in the future?

I shall summarize each one of these programs in terms of the above questions.

These several programs and experiments developed and conducted in various mental hospitals to change the traditional hospital culture and to construct a new hospital culture that would be therapeutically beneficial to patients, proved to be exciting and interesting but in the long run did not appear to bring the results that were hopefully expected. However, they were often productive of certain unintended and unexpected consequences. First, the new therapeutic milieus that were developed in state hospitals tended to provide a cultural climate for patients that often was at marked variance from the family and community cultures from which they came and to which they were discharged. Second, the development of a new therapeutic culture broke up the traditional staff culture, with generally a marked improvement in the morale of the staff. Third, the breakup of traditional patient and staff cultures helped to end the age-old isolation of the mental hospital from the rest of the community. Finally, the new cultural climate produced a reduction in days of hospitalization and emphasized a therapeutic goal of returning the patient to his family and community as quickly as possible.

The consequences of these efforts to construct a therapeutic milieu in the hospital helped to produce a new sensitivity to and a better vision of the parameters of the psychiatric delivery system. This system embraces all the services encompassing both hospital and community which aim to maximize the conditions that will more quickly restore the patient to his normal functioning.

Moreover, the therapeutic milieus developed in selected mental hospitals did help to break the deadening character of the old hospital culture and to elevate the morale of the staff. Thus, in the staff there was a distinct attitude shift from the old helplessness over custodial care to a new hopefulness over the opportunity to use the available therapies. There has been some evidence that the therapeutic milieu has little effect on the chronic mental cases, especially the schizophrenics.[8] The acute cases, in general, respond better, and there has been some indication that the reorganization of wards in the hospital, so that each ward will receive only patients from a given community, seems to speed the social recovery of some patients.[9] However, the test will come if such evidence of patient recovery will continue so that one can recognize that such recoveries are not the consequence of the "halo" effect.

The inauguration of the first community mental health centers almost a decade ago has been described both as the new psychiatric revolution and the greatest mistake that psychiatry ever made.[10] Which view is the most nearly correct, depends not so much on the evidence of therapeutic successes but rather on the expectations of what the centers would accomplish by their establishment. If one expected the mental health centers to contribute to the solution of such perennial problems as war, racial conflict and/or poverty, why then obviously the centers have not been successful. However, if one expected the centers to provide quick and easy access to psychiatric care and treatment for persons in a community, to break down misconceptions about the nature of mental illness, to develop a followup for the treatment plan developed for each patient and to furnish a type of psychiatric intervention that would keep certain patients from ever entering into a mental hospital, then one might argue that by these standards the centers have achieved a modicum of success.

Certainly the centers have symbolized the old ideal of the establishment of small community-based mental hospitals that would provide complete psychiatric services for any person in the community requiring such services. This view has been criticized by those who think that the community mental health center should not be a separate, independent entity, but rather should be woven into the total health care organization of a community.

It is perhaps too soon to give any final judgment as to their total impact on psychiatric theory and practice. Already federal funds for the establishment of new centers have been restricted. Perhaps it is safe to speculate that the continued operation of those centers already established will depend on three factors: the enthusiasm and leadership provided by certain key professionals, the extent to which these professionals can function in a social climate free of political conflict and, finally, the extent to which the centers will continue to receive a broad base of community support. Here, it might be noted that the community mental health centers are likely to make their expected contribution if the psychiatrists attached to them in their diagnostic efforts can develop criteria which will enable them to more clearly distinguish between mental illness, psychological adjustment problems and culturally based deviant behavior. Perhaps it is worth noting that a recent evaluative study of community mental health centers in Finland[11] shows that the wide use of various rehabilitative techniques shortens patient hospital stay and prevents patients from reentering the hospital. They attributed the shortening of the hospital stay largely to the increase of rehabilitative efforts and of outpatient service facilities.

While the idea of community psychiatry has been closely tied to the community mental health center from the beginning, the rationale for this relationship has never been made quite clear. This is so because there has been no clear conception as to the nature of community psychiatry. If community psychiatry refers to psychiatric care and practice as found in the community health center, then the relationship becomes clear. But if community psychiatry implies that the psychiatrist should use his knowledge and expertise to bring about social changes that supposedly would make for a decrease in the incidence of mental disorder and an increase in the number of mentally healthy persons in the community, then the relationship between community psychiatry and the community mental health center is patently unclear.

In this latter guise the psychiatrist leaves his traditional professional role and becomes an agent of social change. If the emphasis on community psychiatry is along this line, it seems very unlikely that psychiatry would be able to survive as a medical specialty. However, psychiatry could continue as a valid medical specialty even though here and there an individual psychiatrist would prefer to exploit the other role. In the former role its survival as a medical specialty seems much more likely and would, in part, depend on the future of the center.

Turning now finally to the future of the early release policy, one might raise the question of how this got started anyway. One certainly suspects the economic motive. By this policy a given state rids itself of a tremendous monetary burden and passes on the responsibility to the local community and the patients' families. Now there is no question in terms of the therapeutic goal that every effort should be made to keep patients out of the hospital. And there would seem to be little doubt that a patient should be discharged from the hospital when he shows that he can assume, even to a limited extent, his roles and his functions in his family and community. But this should not mean that he be returned to the community if he cannot resume his obligations nor that he be placed in surrounding that are less hygienic than those found in the hospital.

Thus one can hardly avoid the conclusion that neither the care nor the recovery of patients has improved under this policy. Rather, what has been achieved is the increase of the number of times a patient is likely to be shuttled back and forth between the hospital and the community. And it seems to be the case, at least in the cities, that when the patient is returned to the community, it is not even likely to be his home community. A continuation of this policy in the long run will lead only to increased social and monetary costs.

There would seem to be no doubt that even though these psychiatric programs have not realized their intended goal, they have been instrumental in directing attention to the very human necessity of providing all persons who develop a mental illness with the best therapy available. The recent legal actions to challenge the authority of the states to hold mental patients involuntarily without providing treatment, attest to this new concern for the mentally ill. The difficulty here, of course, is our lack of knowledge of those therapies that can bring about recovery. Then, too, the recent insistence upon obtaining an informed consent before providing a type of treatment becomes meaningless with a certain type of mental patient. A paranoid patient who has in his delusional system the idea that some people are trying to inject him with heroin so that he can be controlled, will not look with favor upon the physician who wants to inject him with some type of medication. The honest constitutional desire to protect the civil rights of the mental patient has to be balanced with the need to protect the community and at the same time to provide that type of therapy which will control and treat whatever mental disorder the patient has. The policy that will insure the correct therapy for the mental patient and also achieve protection for the community is still in the process of becoming. However, the psychiatric programs examined here have provided experiences useful for shaping such a policy.

In addition, these programs taken collectively, while they have not succeeded in decreasing psychiatric frustration with therapy, have constituted a challenge to those psychiatric views with respect to the significance of sociocultural conditions in the theory and practice of psychiatry. Their continuation in the future will be dependent upon therapeutic results and their value for the education of psychiatrists.

References

1. B. P. Dohrenwend and Barbara S. Dohrenwend, *Social Status and Psychological Disorder: A Causal Inquiry* (New York: Wiley, 1969). Also, A. H. Leighton and J. M. Hughes, "Culture as Causative of Mental Disorder," in *Causes of Mental Disorder: A Review of Epidemiological Knowledge, 1959* (New York: Milbank Memorial Fund, 1961); Lennart Levi, "Stress, Distress and Psychosocial Stimuli," *Occupational Mental Health*, 3 (Fall 1973): pp. 2–10.
2. C. L. Bennett, "The 'Dutchess County Project' for Community Mental Health," *Proceedings of the Third World Congress of Psychiatry*, 3, (Montreal, Canada: McGill and University of Toronto Presses, 1961): 75–78; E. M. Gruenberg, "Can The Reorganization of Psychiatric Services Prevent Some Cases of Social Breakdown?" in A. B. Stokes (ed.) *Psychiatry in Transition* (Toronto: University of Toronto Press, 1967).
3. A. Myerson, "Theory and Principles of the 'Total Push' Method in the Treatment of Chronic Schizophrenics," *American Journal of Psychiatry*, 95 (1939): 1197–1204.
4. Leonard Duhl views early detection as an important preventive measure; see his "Changing Face of Mental Health" published by the Department of Health, Education and Welfare, Washington, D.C., pp. 59–74.

5. O. G. Simmons and N. E. Freeman, "Family Expectations and Post-Hospital Performance of Mental Patients," *Human Relations*, 12 (1959): 233–242; also see G. M. Crocetti and P. V. Lemkau, "Public Opinion of Psychiatric Home Care in an Urban Area," *American Journal of Public Health*, 53 (March 1963): 409–417.

6. Hans R. Huessy, "Some Historical Antecedents of Present American Mental Health Dilemmas," Presented at the Ninth International Congress of Anthropological and Ethnological Sciences, Chicago, Illinois, September 1973.

7. Ruth Benedict, *Patterns of Culture* (Boston: Houghton Mifflin, 1934).

8. G. Tourney, R. Senf, H. W. Dunham, R. S. Glen and J. Gottlieb, "The Effect of Resocialization Techniques on Chronic Schizophrenic Patients," *American Journal of Psychiatry*, 116 (May 1960): 993–1000.

9. C. L. Bennett *op. cit.;* E. M. Gruenberg, *op. cit.*

10. Constance Holden, "Nader on Mental Health Centers: A Movement That Got Bogged Down," *Science*, 77 (1972): 413–415.

11. K. A. Achte and P. Niskanen, "Prognosis in Schizophrenia and Community Psychiatry," *Psychiatrica Fennica*, (1973): 115–122.

—11—

A Psychiatric Afterword

Maxwell Jones, M.D.

I find it very valuable to learn how one sociologist reacts to the present day confusion in the field of community psychiatry; especially when the sociologist has lived through the metamorphosis which has occurred since World War II. I find it hard to disagree with much of what he says and in this sense may not be the best person to give a psychiatrist's reaction to his reaction.

The second paragraph of the author's preface sets the tone for the whole book: "The prevailing uncertainty and vagueness of our knowledge concerning the causes of most mental diseases have made the therapeutic task in psychiatry a most dubious and discouraging procedure. This is reflected in the faddish quality of many types of psychiatric therapy and the tendency for one therapeutic fad to die out as soon as another one puts in an appearance."

The warning that the field of community psychiatry rests on no firm basis in fact, is, in my opinion, fully justified. The need for more evaluative research is evident, but in the meantime exploratory models that can later be studied and evaluated can contribute to the evolution of more exact knowledge. I agree with the author's concern that the present preoccupation with community psychiatry is based on vague theoretical arguments that lack proof. He sees more justification for the development of the community mental health center movement, which he separates from the vague role of the community psychiatrist.

But even the community mental health center movement started when federal monies were made available provided five conditions were met. These conditions insisted that in-patient, out-patient, day hospital, crisis intervention, and consultation and education services should be planned, if a grant application to the National Institute for Mental Health were to be successful. These conditions had no sound foundation in fact and only tended to limit the emergence of new, imaginative models of community mental health care.

Where the community mental health center movement will lead us is far from clear, but it has been a valuable step in our metamorphosis as psychiatrists, forcing us to collaborate much more closely with the other helping professional disciplines, and exposing the need for integrated team work. In some cases the needs of citizens in the neighborhood have been recognized by the establishment of citizen boards with authority over the professional staff, and in even fewer cases has a serious attempt been made to listen to and learn from the consumer.

I would, however, like to attempt to present some positive aspects to offset the thoroughly justified and helpful criticism of both the community psychiatrist and the community mental health centers put forward in this book.[1] To start with, although I would certainly qualify as a member of the community psychiatry fraternity, I feel enriched rather than chastened by the content of this treatise. To me H. Warren Dunham adopts a perfectly legitimate position in relation to community psychiatry although he does seem largely to ignore the significant contribution that his own world of behavioral science has made to improving the very situation he describes so powerfully.

Take, for instance, the development of a therapeutic culture in relation to mental hospitals aspiring to a milieu approach. These have been largely inspired by mental health professionals who in the main were uninfluenced by the developments in the behavioral sciences. The training of psychiatrists up to now has generally ignored such subjects as learning theory, systems theory, and communication theory. Further, the role of the doctor as leader in a therapeutic team has been largely unchallenged.

The emphasis on social organization, which has characterized my writing[2,3,4,5] and practice, established as early as 1947 the concept of a therapeutic community with a therapeutic culture. This culture aimed at the establishment of a value system growing out of the interaction between patients and staff and deviated markedly from the traditional medical authority system.

Systems theory as such did not exist at that time, and it was our lack of an effective treatment modality for treating character disorders that led to our initial attempts to establish a social environment that would allow social learning to occur. Our goal was to supply an environment where the social interaction associated with "normal" growth could be experienced by individuals who had missed out on it as a result of broken homes and the absence of caring parents as models. In the foreword to my first book,[1] Aubrey Lewis, then Professor of Psychiatry at the Maudsley Hospital in London, implied some concern at my transfer of training from the scientific field to one of "social engineering." For me the break from traditional (academic) psychiatry was not, as H. Warren Dunham implies, due to disenchantment with current methods of treatment in schizophrenia or other mental diseases. In fact I had been in charge of the physical treatment unit at the Maudsley Hospital and felt the excitement associated with the introduction of insulin coma, continuous narcosis, abreactive techniques, shock treatments, etc. What effected a change in my attitude to traditional psychiatry were the relative neglect of the patient as a person and the high priority given to teaching and research. I wanted to be associated with a hospital practice where the needs of the patient came first.

Another factor in my evolution in the direction

of community psychiatry was being given the responsibility in 1940 for a psychosomatic unit (called the Effort Syndrome Unit) of 100 beds where soldiers from the British Armed Forces with cardiac neuroses were treated. These five war years opened my eyes to the possibility of using the patients' peers as effective change agents in collaboration with the professional staff. The results of this experiment, while not conclusive, suggest something more positive than Dunham's skepticism about the results of treatment outside the formal categories of mental illness. The social structure of this psychosomatic unit in 1944 might be summarized as follows:[6]

1. An attempt was being made to think of treatment as a continuous process operating throughout the entire waking life of the patient while in hospital. The therapeutic interview with the doctor did not alone constitute treatment, while the organization of the rest of the day was being left largely to chance. The patient was reacting to the hospital community in much the same way that he reacted to communities outside. We began to think that a study of these real life situations might be expected to give more information about the nature of the patient's problems, than personal history recounted under the highly artificial conditions of an office interview.

2. In order to make such observation possible, a reorganization of the hospital society was needed with a greater degree of social penetration between the three main sub-groups, pa-

tients, nurses and doctors. Thus the original hospital hierarchy was broken down and free communication between doctors, nurses and patients established. The daily discussion between the entire patient population, nurses and doctors and the continuous growth of meetings between various sub-groups, e.g., nurses' tutorials, all aided this process. It is doubtful if the rapid metamorphosis which we witnessed, could have occurred in peacetime; hospital traditions are strong. However, we were helped by the temporary nature of the hospital and of the nurses aides who were drawn from other professions, together with the general tendency to change which was apparent in many spheres during war-time.

3. Along with the growing awareness of the importance of the communal roles of the doctors and nurses, in addition to their more specific therapeutic functions, the patients' role in the hospital society was being scrutinized. From the early part of the war Dr. Aubrey Lewis had stressed the importance of vocational selection in patients returning to Army duties. The introduction of Army personnel officers by the Army authorities soon met this need. Considerably less than half of the patients from the Effort Syndrome Unit were discharged from the Army direct from hospital, and despite the favourable labour market which existed during the war, vocational guidance was of great importance with this group if unnecessary stresses in civilian life were to be avoided. To aid the transition from Army to

civilian life we began to explore the possibilities of infiltration into the local community, and an arrangement was made with the local technical college to teach typewriting, engineering, etc., to selected groups of patients from Mill Hill Emergency Hospital.

In the psychosomatic unit our initial concern was with the physiological responses to physical stress as related to the symptoms of palpitation, breathlessness, left chest pain, postural giddiness, fainting and fatigue. Ultimately our treatment was essentially educational, helping the peer group to understand the meaning of their symptoms and using audiovisual aids and open discussion with the whole group of 100 armed forces personnel.

Dunham frequently makes the point that treatment in psychiatry is at the mercy of fads and fashion, as we do not have sufficient information about causation to be specific. But in our psychosomatic unit the physiological mechanism of symptom production was largely understood as a result of our own research.[7] We had learned that no medical pathology was involved, and the symptoms were related to failure of homeostasis. This information helped us to convince most of the subjects that they did not have heart disease (as they feared), but merely had a relatively poor response to exercise. Our sharing of this information with the subjects (many of whom had participated as subjects in the research), and our discussion of the findings with them had a powerful influence in changing their attitude towards their bodily functioning.

Circumstance again conspired to push me in the direction of community psychiatry when in May, 1945, I was seconded from the Maudsley Hospital to run a 300-bed unit in Dartford, Kent for returned prisoners of war from the British Armed Forces in Europe and the Far East.

The prisoner of war unit now presented a sociological rather than a physiological problem. The returned soldiers referred to us were among the most emotionally disturbed of the 100,000 British troops who came back to the United Kingdom at the end of the war. Again we had a relatively homogeneous group of casualties whose symptoms were related to their captivity (up to five years) sometimes under conditions of extreme deprivation. They lacked food, clothing, warmth, exercise and information from the outside world:

> During the eleven months the Unit was in being, twelve hundred patients were dealt with, the average length of stay in hospital being six to eight weeks. Each block of fifty men rapidly became a small community with its four wards forming smaller sub-groups; the social structure of these communities followed the pattern of the Effort Syndrome Unit at Mill Hill. Daily talks were held in each block and the mechanisms of psychosomatic symptoms were discussed on two mornings; on the third morning a documentary film was shown followed by a discussion. These films covered such topics as day nurseries, rehabilitation and job training. A fourth morning was devoted to psychodrama

followed by a discussion. The fifth morning was used for a discussion with the patients about problems affecting the hospital community.

The major sociological development at Dartford occurred in our relations with the local community, the opportunity for such developments being particularly favourable. The war had just ended and public sentiment was very friendly towards the ex-prisoner-of-war; the men were still in uniform and their presence soon became known to the majority of the population of Dartford. Our aim was to find social and vocational roles in the local community for these patients while they were still in hospital. This was clearly desirable with patients (provided they were well enough to assume such roles) who had been excluded from normal society for periods of up to five years. Besides speaking at local rotary clubs and the like, I made personal contact with numerous firms, shops and farms. Our problem was explained to them and we ultimately had the active support of over seventy employers. The work available represented a good cross-section of the employments in a small industrial and rural community; the range of choice included farming, dairy farming, market-gardening, building, engineering (both agricultural and general), clerical work, and work in foundries, shipyards, paper mills, chemical factories, printing firms, and numerous small shops. The big factories offered many specialized jobs, e.g. work in electrical maintenance, heating, progress, print room, shipping offices, etc. In this way we built up a potential employment field for our total patient population.

The Government put at our disposal three large buses, which, following separate itineraries, dropped the patients each morning and afternoon at their different occupations, and collected them again two hours later. Naturally some of the patients were too ill to be sent out on what we came to call work therapy, and a carpentry shop was available in the hospital for these patients. A nurse was employed full time supervising the attendances at work therapy and acting as liaison between myself and the employers. Patients were allowed to change their occupations as often as they wished. The psychologist came to find this reality testing in actual work-situation more useful than any other forms of vocational test.

A written follow-up study[8] done three and a half months following discharge by the Ministry of Labour showed that of 687 patients discharged during the period July to December, 1945, 610 (90 per cent) were reported as being in work or training, 31 not yet in work, and 8 unfit for work.

I have mentioned these two early experiments carried out between the years 1940 and 1947 because while they may not refute much of Dunham's argument, they do at least highlight the great difference between the slow evolution of community psychiatry in the United Kingdom, as compared with the U.S. Federal Government's unilateral decision to foster and finance the development of community psychiatry as early as 1961.[9]

This brings me to my major point of disagreement with Dunham, which relates to his almost total disregard for the concept of social learning.[10] By this I mean two-way communication motivated by some inner need or stress leading to the overt or covert expression of feeling and involving cognitive processes and change. The term implies a change in the individual's attitudes and/or beliefs as a result of the experience. These changes are incorporated and modify his personality and self-image. Dunham admits that a democratic sociocultural environment can be created within a mental health facility that will improve staff morale, which in turn might benefit the patient although not necessarily insuring his recovery. Further, he sees community psychiatry as expanding the parameters of mental illness to include various social problem areas resulting in the individual's maladjustment to life, e.g., juvenile delinquency, crime, drug addiction, and the like.

I agree that the goals of community psychiatry may far exceed our knowledge, so that to plan, let alone treat, social casualties may be beyond our reach at present. But this is a good reason why various approaches, including sociocultural environmental studies, have some validity.

My own evolution as a community psychiatrist stems from the early experiences I have already outlined. As systems theory[11] and organization development[12] emerged in the past decade, however, it became evident that the therapeutic community principles which we had slowly and painfully conceived since 1940 were very similar. Thus the prime importance of two-way communication of ideas and feelings at all levels of the system, shared decision making, and learning as a social process, were all seen as active ingredients of any system for change.

For me the concept of a therapeutic community has moved from the hospital setting to include community mental health programs. Thus while on the staff at Oregon State Hospital, in Salem, Oregon (1959 to 1962), we developed county units which brought psychiatric services to local communities. For seven years (1962–1969) I was physician-superintendent of a mental hospital in Scotland. This gave me the power to sanction change from a traditional authority structure to a therapeutic community model (or an open system to use a more generic term). As the open system evolved in the hospital, it seemed inevitable that our service area should expand into the catchment area which we served. Three county teams linked up with the 68 family doctors serving a population of 100,000 people. My clinical role was focused mainly on geriatric and chronic schizophrenic patients who would certainly fit into Dunham's categories of the mentally ill. However, an open systems approach seemed as relevant to the treatment of schizophrenics as to my work in the community with the emotionally disturbed and family crises.

In other words, I was not turning away from the treatment of the mentally ill because of their limited response to treatment, and instead seeking more "treatable" emotionally disturbed individuals in the community. But like every psychiatrist visiting a schizophrenic in his home setting to make an initial assessment of the family system, I was learning much about how the social environment appeared to contribute to the family disorganization and the emergence of an identified patient. Dunham's contention that this may not represent a specific treatment modality is probably true, but what treatment approach *has* proved its success with this type of patient?

The fact is that a systems approach at least offers some clues as to what supportive system should take the place of the family or other system which has failed. In this context the work of Fairweather[13] seems highly relevant. Many schizophrenics who have become isolated (institutionalized) in psychiatric facilities can be helped by the formation of an "intentional family." Two to four patients who seem to accept each other are helped to have frequent opportunities to interact, to go on shopping expeditions, learn housekeeping, etc., and then given a supervised living situation for a few months before moving into an apartment of their own. In this way their psychoses may be contained, even if their distortion of reality remains.

Finally, while deploring the trend to empty state hospitals before there is an appropriate plan for their treatment in the community, Dunham offers no solution to make the community mental health centers more effective in treating psychotics.

As a consultant (change agent) I have been privileged to see many of these centers, and with few exceptions they openly admit their incompetence to deal with these institutionalized ex-patients. Their professional staffs have in most cases had little exposure to this type of patient and tend to prefer the more "treatable" early psychotic referrals.

One major difficulty with the "chronic" patient in the community is that the passive dependency often presumed to be a by-product of hospitalization makes regular medication (mandatory for most schizophrenics) difficult to maintain. The community mental health centers seem to expect the patient to visit them for his medication, and home visiting of every needy chronic patient in the community on a regularly scheduled basis may overtax their resources.

It would seem that there are at least two alternatives that would meet this problem; either the centers themselves could assume this responsibility to identify and treat every chronic patient in their catchment area; or the state hospital could assume responsibility for its former institutionalized chronic patients. In practice I have seen both systems work satisfactorily, but where the centers are concerned the professional staff has had little or no past experience with such patients in mental hospitals. As far as I know, no center claims to have a complete inventory of this type of patient in the community, or to have a follow-up service for all such ex-patients.

Fort Logan Mental Health Center in Denver, Colorado is a unique state hospital in the sense that since its initiation 13 years ago it has aimed at preventing the onset of the institutional syndrome. With an able and relatively numerous professional staff the center hoped that its therapeutic community approach would avoid the onset of chronicity. With fewer than 300 beds for a population of approximately one million, it has not realized its goal, and 2 per cent of the patients referred have come to show a passive-dependent picture very similar to chronic institutionalized patients from the larger and less well-staffed state hospitals.

A serious attempt to supervise and treat the ex-patient has been undertaken at Fort Logan by forming a special department called Tertiary Aid and Prevention (T.A.P.).[14] This team of eight professionals drawn from the regular staff is responsible for the care of approximately 140 ex-patients. These patients are housed mainly in boarding homes and family care homes, and the staff is available 24 hours a day to respond to any crisis situation.

Thus the evidence to date would seem to indicate that as yet the majority of the centers have neither the experience nor the inclination to assume responsibility for chronic patients in their catchment areas. In the interim it would seem logical to use state hospital staff to follow up and supervise discharged chronic patients in the community. Such a move gives variety and interest to the stressful and often monotonous role of the hospital mental health worker. Nor need this plan lead to a clash with the community mental health center staff who usually welcome such an arrangement.

Let us now examine the second assumption that boarding homes, nursing homes and other hospital alternatives are an improvement on the "back wards" of state hospitals. I have written elsewhere on this topic but it seems that many patients discharged from state hospitals are seriously neglected. Recently I visited Santa Clara County Aftercare Services project in San Jose, California. There are 78 official board and care homes listed, which serve approximately 1,300 clients who are mentally ill or retarded. The majority of these were former patients in Agnew State Hospital, which has been completely closed down in line with the current policy in California. These homes are either quite small, with 6 to 12 residents, or larger, with 20 to 50 residents, and all are run for profit by untrained operators.

This system of aftercare is by its very nature counter-rehabilitative. An overwhelming number of residents are on welfare and have no supportive system to turn to—no family, no friends, and since its closure, no state hospital. The operators of the homes are dependent on the residents for their source of income. Nor can they afford to employ much untrained help of even a mediocre quality. These were the circumstances which led the Santa Clara County Health Department Mental Health Services to obtain a grant and establish a Board and Care Consultation Unit.

This Unit employs eight mental health professionals whose aim is to help the board and care homes to improve their rehabilitative, social and medical services and if possible lead to a more productive and independent way of life for the patients outside the homes. It is too early to comment on the results of this project, but the resistance of the bulk of operators to mental health training is epitomized by the turnout at a much publicized afternoon workshop, where approximately 10 per cent of the operators appeared! To be fair, this sample seemed to think positively and had a degree of internal commitment which promised well for the future.

Two days later we had an all day conference sponsored by the Greater Bay Area Conference of Local Mental Health Directors. The attendance of 450 community care workers communicated in an unmistakable way that they were angry, confused, and feeling relatively helpless. They were all involved in attempting to cope with the mass of passive-dependent mostly ex-mental hospital patients who were now their responsibility. California by 1973 had reduced its 1955 in-patient population of 50,000 to 7,000 and shifted the responsibility to the counties. The resulting anxiety and virtual chaos were articulated by everyone who spoke at the workshop.

Having indicated that the present tendency to close the existing state hospitals or drastically reduce their population (558,900 in 1955 reduced to 248,600 in 1973 for the entire country) has resulted in no demonstrable benefit to many chronic ex-state hospital patients. Let us now consider what can be done to improve matters.

At one extreme Massachusetts[15] has decided to eliminate its existing 10 remaining mental hospitals over a period of five years and consign its 7,000 inpatients to the tender mercies of "the community." The economic argument is strong, as the state hospi-

tals' budget for 1972 was 80 million dollars. Moreover, as in most states, this represented the lion's
share of monies available for other mental health
services, including community mental health centers
(in Massachusetts, 80 per cent compared with 20 per
cent). The Massachusetts plan shows a remarkable
degree of faith in the value of extending community
mental health services as at present understood, to
encompass all the mentally ill in the state. Un-
deterred by what has happened to the ex-mental
hospital patients in California, New York, and most
other states, Massachusetts plans a fairly orthodox
community mental health program, the transition to
be spread over a period of five years. Nevertheless
the Massachusetts plan represents a most valuable
pilot project which should yield some much needed
data. It is a plan that allows for gradual change and
avoids the haste and absence of planning that has
characterized so much of the community psychiatry
action to date. It mobilizes the budget spent on the
state hospitals and transfers this to finance its community program and presumably gains independence from the vagaries of federal funding.

By creating 39 catchment areas, each with its
own director, it establishes relatively small population areas where integration of services may be possible, and above all it implies state funding for hospital
alternatives. This seems to me to be the one original
aspect of the plan, and the one aspect that gets away
from the dangers inherent in the running of such
facilities for gain by private enterprise. Massachusetts currently provides accommodation for 479 ex-

patients and hopes that by 1975 it will have accommodation for an additional 2,000 transitional patients.

Less impressive are the plans for redeploying the 9,000 personnel who are at present employed in the Massachusetts state hospitals. This is to be accomplished by a combination of personnel relocation, attrition, and retraining. It would be interesting to hear what the personnel have to say to this plan, especially those employees who have worked for many years with chronic patients. Plans for early retirement are envisaged, but this gives little impression of the misery ahead for many employees. Inservice training for community work will probably attract only the younger, more flexible staff, who may also be expected to be less rooted to their homes in the vicinity of existing state hospitals. A small minority will probably find satisfaction in further opportunities to work with chronic patients in the community.

But the major criticism I would raise is the tacit assumption that we know how to handle chronic patients in the community or even know what community psychiatry really is. The Massachusetts plan will certainly add to our knowledge in this field.

I would now like to go to the other extreme and question if the state hospital has served its purpose and should now disappear. Having been the physician-superintendent of a mental hospital for seven years (Dingleton Hospital, in Melrose, Scotland from 1962 to 1969) and now serving on the staff at Fort Logan Mental Health Center, the state mental hospital for Denver, Colorado, I have a feeling that the majority of state hospitals in the United States were doomed from the start. Even though conditions for patients in the state hospitals are in general improving, there has been no attempt to effect the radical changes that could transform these hospitals and overcome many of the negative characteristics conveyed by the word "institutionalized."

Society sought to avoid the unpleasant reality of mental illness by isolating and insulating people deemed to be "sick." The idea of pathology dominated the thinking of professionals and general public alike. The "sick" person could best be ministered to by the medical profession and the helping professions generally. So we got mental *hospitals* and the expensive medical professionals dominated the scene.

Economic needs were met by buying ground cheaply in outlying areas and building huge residential establishments. The physical environment and the food were usually the cheapest available. All this is old hat, and there is no need to elaborate how almost inevitably the environmental, social, and economic forces all conspired to create the negative image of the "snakepit."

By assuming the relatively powerful role of superintendent of a mental hospital in Scotland I was in a position to sanction change and operate as a change agent myself. We were able to develop an open system[16,17,18,19] both intra- and extramurally so that the mental health needs of a population of 100,000 were adequately met. The therapeutic community principles of two-way communication at all levels of patients and staff, shared decision making, and learning as a social process were established through time. Much the same principles apply at Fort Logan (1961–1974), which, although a new model for a state hospital, has, as far as I know, had no imitators, although it has profoundly influenced the thinking of many mental health professionals in the United States. At both Dingleton and Fort Logan the extramural dimension, i.e., community psychiatry, has had as much attention as in-patient psychiatry. However, the development of community mental health centers in the Denver area has limited Fort Logan's community involvement, and caused it to focus increasingly on the *chronic* patient in the hospital and in the community.

This brief account of the two extreme positions —the one stressing the absorption of chronic patients in a community based program, and the other the complementarity between a mental hospital run as an open system and the community into which it extends its services—in no way precludes many other models. The development of mental hospitals as open systems implies the disappearance of the preoccupation with pathology and a new trend in the direction of a village settlement, with far fewer medically trained professionals. Thus the spectrum from hospital to half-way house, to boarding home, to family care, intentional families,[20] and various other hospital alternatives such as the crisis hostel,[21] to full employment outside, becomes a challenge more of social change and flexible systems than of "sickness" hospitalization, and treatment.

To close down existing state hospitals may be the logical step toward a more accepting attitude by the general public regarding the chronic mentally ill. But first let us be clear about our objectives. Does the present pattern of community psychiatry as exemplified by the community mental health centers deal adequately with the chronic ex-mental patients when they are extruded from the state hospitals? Have we any sound knowledge about the possibility of creating a positive public attitude toward these social casualties, or are we still as prejudiced on this issue as we were two decades ago?[22] Do we know enough about hospital alternatives to know which of the various models will be appropriate for any one particular case? What are the relative advantages and disadvantages of state—as opposed to private— ownership of these facilities? What do we mean by *training* in community psychiatry, particularly as most of the mental health professionals are trained in universities that still remain relatively remote from the social, economic, ethnic, cultural and ecological problems of the underprivileged areas where most mental illness develops? What roles and role relationships are optimal between professionals, nonprofessionals (indigenous workers), volunteers, and the patients themselves? Finally, can the existing state hospitals be transformed into some form of social system appropriate to the needs of the most severe social casualties?

I would like to conclude by elaborating on this last point. My own experience at Dingleton and Fort

Logan has convinced me that a state hospital need not be a drab, dull establishment, defeated by the apparently hopeless task of rehabilitating the hard core of chronic patients, including the geriatric and brain damaged populations. To dilute the problem by discharging this severely handicapped minority of patients into the community has relatively little chance of success.

There are many ways of creating a positive climate in such establishments, including the following:

1. Forget the word "hospital" and develop an open system including a functional role for the residents commensurate with their capacities.
2. Develop the latent potential in residents and staff so that there is a feeling of growth throughout the entire community.
3. Limit the size of such "open systems" to less than 400, which may mean decentralized units in larger establishments.
4. Explore the optimal culture (attitudes, beliefs, and values) for such a facility and develop a therapeutic culture that may differ markedly from the culture outside.
5. Activities should aim to interest and satisfy the emotional and intellectual needs of everyone—thus a percussion band and community singing might please and socially involve the aged, while the "out of favour" farm might satisfy many chronic schizophrenics, especially in a rural area.

6. Groups might lose much of their present sinister qualities and form spontaneously around a crisis situation. Or chronic patients might feel comfortable and communicate more in a bar-like atmosphere over a (small) beer!
7. With such a social structure as a base, other relevant treatment modalities such as reparenting,[23] behavior modification, transactional analysis, etc., might be added.
8. Finally, such an open system might come to be partly self-supporting through sheltered workshops, market gardening, etc., and take on many of the characteristics of a village settlement.

FOOTNOTES

1. Many other psychiatrists have made similar contributions but will not be noted here, as they are already included in Dunham's material.
2. M. Jones, *Social Psychiatry* (London: Tavistock Publications, 1952). Published in the U.S. as *The Therapeutic Community.* (N.Y.: Basic Books, 1953).
3. M. Jones, *Social Psychiatry, in the Community, in Hospitals, and in Prisons* (Springfield, Ill.: Charles C Thomas, 1962).
4. M. Jones, *Social Psychiatry in Practice* (N.Y.: Penguin Books, 1968).

5. M. Jones, *Beyond the Therapeutic Community* (New Haven: Yale U. Press, 1968).
6. M. Jones, *Social Psychiatry. Op. cit.,* pp. 14–15.
7. M. Jones, *Physiological and Psychological Responses to Stress in Neurotic Patients.* This treatise, submitted for an M.D. at Edinburgh University, was awarded a Gold Medal. Our work was largely confirmed by similar studies carried out at Harvard Fatigue Laboratory during the war.
8. M. Jones, *Social Psychiatry. Op. cit.,* pp. 23–24.
9. Joint Commission on Mental Illness & Health, *Action for Mental Health* (N.Y.: Basic Books, 1961).
10. M. Jones, *Beyond the Therapeutic Community. Op. cit.*
11. C. Argyris, *Intervention Theory & Method.* (Reading, Mass.: Addison-Wesley, 1970).
12. W. G. Bennis, *Organization Development.* (Reading, Mass.: Addison-Wesley, 1969).
13. G. W. Fairweather, *et al. Community Life for the Mentally Ill: An Alternative to Institutional Care* (Chicago: Aldine, 1969).
14. M. Kincheloe, and L. Hagar, *Out the Back Wards Door.* Unpublished. Available from Mrs. Hagar (12453 W. Tennessee Pl., Lakewood, Colorado 80228) for $3.00, this is an excellent account of the type of treatment carried out by the T.A.P. program.
15. *Community Mental Health and the Mental Hospital.* Final Report of the Massachusetts Mental

Hospital Planning Project. Available from UCPC (14 Somerset St., Boston, Massachusetts 02108) for $2.00.

16. M. Jones, *Beyond the Therapeutic Community. Op. cit.*

17. M. Jones, "From Hospital to Community Psychiatry," *Community Mental Health Journal,* 6 (1970):187–195.

18. M. Jones, "Psychiatry, Systems Theory, Education & Change," *British Journal of Psychiatry,* 124 (1974):75–80.

19. P. Polak and M. Jones, "The Psychiatric Nonhospital, A Model for Change," *Community Mental Health Journal,* 9 (1973):123–132.

20. G. W. Fairweather, *et al. Op. cit.*

21. B. D. Brook, "Crisis Hostel, an Alternative to Psychiatric Hospitalization for Emergency Patients," *Hospital & Community Psychiatry,* 24 (1973):621–624.

22. E. Cumming, and J. Cumming, *Closed Ranks,* (Cambridge, Mass.: Harvard University Press 1957).

23. J. Schiff, and B. Day, *All My Children* (N.Y.: Pyramid Publications, 1970).

—12—

A Sociological Afterword

ELAINE CUMMING, PH.D.

Criticizing a book like this is difficult for a number of reasons. First, there is the problem of overcoming the gratuitous advantage gained by the passage of time. The earliest of these chapters was written in 1956 when the enthusiasms current among mental health professionals were quite different from today's. Time alone has made some of these enthusiasms ridiculous, and it is tempting to say that although Dunham saw then how ridiculous they were, he was much too gentle with them. It is easy to forget that almost no one else criticized them at all.

A second difficulty facing the critic is the particular role that Dunham was playing when he was asked to write these papers and give these talks. Any social scientist whose researches shatter tradition as did Dunham's early epidemiological studies is bound to be asked for his opinions on a number of practical matters. Although such invitations to act as a social critic are forthcoming because of prior scholarly production, the role itself is not a scholarly one, but is rather that of a concerned citizen with a particular expertise. Dunham's training by the great "second generation" of sociologists at Chicago prepared him well for this role alternation. Robert Faris has summed up the Chicago tradition thus:

> An objective science does not concern itself immediately with welfare. In order to be efficient it must be disinterested. But science, or knowledge, is always in the service of ends, and the ultimate justification of science, certainly the science of human nature, will be the service it can render to human welfare.[1]

These writings must, then, be criticized as what they are: critical analyses of what may be roughly called the mental health movement of the 1950s and 1960s.

For me, however, the greatest difficulty in criticizing these pieces arises from the fact that Dunham's career has so closely paralleled my own that most of my criticisms of his work could be exactly mirrored by criticisms he might make of mine. Figuratively speaking, we look at one another from glass houses. There are, of course, specific points at which the work might be faulted, just as there are points at which it is difficult not to break into cheers. But I shall focus particularly on the consequences of Dunham's tendency to use "culture" as his organizing principle, while noting in passing his tendency—which he shares with me—to surround himself with the work of others sympathetic to his viewpoint, or known to him, thus failing to hear other important voices.

"Culture" versus "Structure"

The concept of culture as an organizing principle has the merits of humanity and complexity. Furthermore, as a concept it subsumes such important variables as the norms and values that inform action in a social system. Unfortunately, it is hard to decompose the concept of culture, and difficult, if not impossible, to operationalize it. Because culture dominates Dunham's general approach to all his subjects, he is especially sensitive to such important matters as attitudes and ideology, but relatively insensitive to such issues as organizational structure. Social structure as an alternative organizing concept in turn yields insights different from those yielded by culture. In the next few pages, I will suggest some of the things that Dunham might have noticed over the years if he had used structure as his organizing critical concept, always keeping in mind, however, that no one can do everything and that what he did do has been of unique value.

Therapeutic Environments

The earliest modern attempts to manipulate hospital environments in a therapeutic way met with indifference or hostility from much of the psychiatric establishment at the same time that they were embraced with evangelical fervor by a few zealots. True to his tradition, Dunham greeted the ferment accompanying the idea of the therapeutic environment with a proper skepticism and some very sensible suggestions about the integrative role of the environment in the multipronged attack upon the patient's illness (See Chapters 2 and 3). Nevertheless, the concept of culture was too general to allow him to see clearly that beneath the general rubric, several very different kinds of programs were being instituted. The radically egalitarian therapeutic community of Maxwell Jones, which Dunham's approach was ideal for describing, was only one of the various programs being proposed. Dunham, as critic, rightly observed from the beginning that the therapeutic community was flawed by Utopianism and hence by a disjunction with everyday life. He did not, however, make a distinction between this type of intervention and the prescribed environments developed at Topeka and doomed to extinction, probably as a result of the impossibility of carrying them out, nor did he distinguish it from the structured environments pioneered at Chestnut Lodge,[2] developed in other kinds of settings,[3] and finally absorbed into the psychiatric mainstream.*

*Another branch of environmental manipulation based on various psychological paradigms had hardly begun to emerge at that time, but has since dominated much hospital intervention in the guise of token economies, behavior modification, and so on. I would like to hear Dunham's views of these.

I have suggested elsewhere that these interventions can be divided into two classifications: those aimed primarily at changing the individual, and those aimed at helping him to cope with everyday life in spite of his deficits,[4] but there are no doubt other and better ways to classify them. My point is that while Dunham's cultural framework allowed him to see the unity in all these therapeutic activities very clearly, perhaps it obscured from him their diversity and consequently blunted his critical impact.

One of the most admirable things about Dunham's work is his steady insistence on respect for the facts of the matter. All through the height of the enthusiasm for therapeutic environments, and through the various other enthusiasms he discusses as well, he never forgot to remind his listeners that those facts that we have (and some of them we have courtesy of Dunham himself) suggest that some serious mental illness is biologically based and that there is no reason to believe that the environment will have any profound effect upon it at all. It took courage in those days to suggest that such facts be taken into consideration, because biological causation was being looked upon as defeatist and even reactionary by many psychiatrists, whose concepts of social causation were leading to a belief in social therapies. Among the most enthusiastic social practitioners there grew up a faith in one therapy for all illnesses: membership in the therapeutic community. It was this distinctly nonmedical orientation that Dunham questioned persistently and effectively.

Mental Health Centers

During the enthusiasm for mental health centers that swept across the United States in the 1960s, Dunham's skepticism subsided somewhat, but not sufficiently to prevent him from raising awkward questions (Dunham is at his best when he is raising questions). He asked whether there was a danger that the centers' staff members would select for their attention only those with interesting and tractable illnesses and foresaw that there would be more and more patients with less and less wrong with them for psychiatrists to choose among as the range of behaviors defined as deviant widened. He asked whether the chronic schizophrenic, who is at the heart of the psychiatric matter, would be neglected, and he asked whether the centers' staffs would fritter away their time on the latest fads, prevention, and consultation. He even asked whether the centers would shirk the job of rehabilitation (Chapter 4). All of these were good questions, and much of what he feared would happen did happen, for although the centers had a firm base in the most helpful cultural attitudes that had so far been seen, they had structural features that as good as guaranteed that they would succumb to the temptations pointed out by Dunham.

I think an argument can be made[5] that the mental health centers contained in their very mandate a denial of everything then known about chronic mental illness, particularly schizophrenia. They were organized around the treatment of acute illness, not disability. Although crisis intervention was among their five primary functions, rehabilitation was an optional secondary function. In other words, a mental health center could receive federal funding without offering rehabilitation services. No wonder almost no one did. Indeed, it is doubtful if the mental health centers were ever suitable for treating any category of illness except neurosis, for which they were not needed because of the abundant supply of private psychiatrists and outpatient clinics, and depression, a disease that afflicts the most interesting and least refractory of the psychotic group. Not only were there mental health centers organized around crisis intervention rather than around rehabilitation, but they almost all put limits on the length of stay in their inpatient services. They seemed to be saying, "If you are acutely ill and will get well quickly, we will treat you, but if not, you must go elsewhere." It is not surprising that like the outpatient clinics before them, they created a clientele for themselves that excluded the hard-core, chronic patients whether they were schizophrenics, character disorders, dementias associated with brain disorder, or anything else.

A further look at the mandate of these centers suggests another reason why they were unlikely ever to attack the hard cases. As Dunham rightly points out, it is only natural for a doctor to want to treat patients whom he feels he can help, and provisions for funding made no stipulation that centers accept responsibility for comprehensive service to a defined population. Although the concept of "a catchment area" was derived from services in other countries, the crucial element of responsibility was missing. The most that was asked of these centers was that they see a reasonable proportion of "service cases," and, of course, there was nothing to prevent these service cases from having interesting illnesses. At the end of 1968, H. G. Whittington was discussing catchment areas at a conference called to evaluate the status of the mental health centers:

> ... there is no reward system for the people who might be willing to take care of chronic patients in the community. The state keeps most of the money to run the state hospitals. The community programs are left with what NIMH hands out, which isn't enough to do anything significant for the bulk of the chronic schizophrenic population. The public morality says it's a fine idea; the private morality of money doesn't work that way.[6]

Perhaps the mental health center should be viewed as a compromise between the psychiatric establishment and society. During the period covered by Dunham's essays, the high-prestige establishment was composed of the members of psychiatric faculties of medical schools, private practitioners, and certain federal civil servants with policy making and money granting powers. This group had been criticized for years because its psychoanalytic orientation had led to the neglect of the chronic psychotic patient, and while the mental health center widened its scope enough to include the most treatable and attractive psychotics, it did not open wide enough to include the difficult schizophrenics.

At the heart of all these issues lies the unanswered question, whose side is the psychiatrist on? Although Dunham recognizes the question and discusses it, I am not sure that I agree with his solution. If a psychiatrist takes on a chronically ill patient for treatment, is he not managing that patient rather than treating him? Dunham refers, on a number of occasions, to the dangers of acting as "an agent of social control." I completely sympathize with his protest against psychiatry's defining the whole world as a clinic and itself as the clinician, but the problem of when a doctor, in the course of doing his medical duty, must act as an agent of society, needs to be met head on. What about organic brain disease? What about chronic schizophrenia? Both of these illnesses require management or guidance rather than treatment, and yet if the doctor deserts them because he refuses to be an agent of social control, who will care for their victims and how will we prevent them from being second-class sick people? If a psychiatrist urges his schizophrenic patient to go to work, is he acting for the patient or for the norms, or both? What if he gets a social worker to urge the patient to get a job? Is the medical role not often at the interface between the individual and society? Can it be otherwise?[7]

Dunham appears to have a firm position on these points, but these papers do not happen to explicate it. I suspect that this is because he summarizes his attitude as confidence in the "medical model." Unfortunately, this phrase has as many meanings as users. Some people, especially those who are involved in the design of health care programs, use the word to refer to the hierarchical relationships between doctors, nurses, and other paramedical staff. Scheff[8] refers to the medical model as a "competitor" with labeling theory as though the medical model were a theory of behavior. In both examples, the meaning of the phrase is ambiguous or even obscure to the uninitiated reader. Dunham sounds as though he had assigned a rational meaning to this overworked phrase; I wish he had defined it.

Community Psychiatry

Over the excesses that marked the brief, passionate, and one-sided love affair of a few strategically placed psychiatrists with "communities," a veil should be drawn. It is worth noting in passing, however, that while the idea of the therapeutic environment was developed by doctors trying to solve problems in the practice of psychiatry, the idea of community psychiatry was hatched in university departments and government agencies not primarily concerned with patient care. This may be one reason why the first was ultimately absorbed into psychiatric practice while the other was quickly forgotten.

Dunham was not alone in his dismay at the claims of psychiatrists to treat the "sick community," but there were not nearly as many voices as there should have been. It is salutory to read here some of the quotations from the zealots of the time alongside Dunham's indignant but always rational protests.

There is a question that remains to be raised, however: how did it happen? Was it entirely "retreat from patients?"[9] Was it to increase the status of the specialty? What is the relationship between this emergence of medicine in general, and psychiatry in particular, as a kind of reform branch of the professional community, and the assumption of a leadership role by clergymen during the civil rights movement and later on by lawyers on behalf of the poor and those deprived of their civil liberties? The topic of medical man as reformer or as member of an influential élite group in society is not addressed by Dunham. I hope we will hear from him on this subject in the future.

It is in Dunham's trenchant criticisms of community psychiatry that I become most aware of the separate streams of social science in which he and I swim, in spite of our similar interests and outlooks. There are references in his work that I am embarrassed not to have known before, yet that most effective of iconoclasts, Barbara Wootten, is missing.[10]

A quick check of Dunham's seventy or so references against approximately the same number in five of my own publications directed to the same general topic yielded only four identical items. I was able to find eight more references that were to the same author but different works. This is a sobering fact. There is always the possibility that the field is so broad and the output so vast that it is impossible to cover anything like all of it, but my guess is that Dunham and I do not differ greatly from most social scientists in that many of our references reflect our place of training, our theoretical "school," our work career, and even our individual tastes and predilections rather than the best evidence available.

The Early Release of Schizophrenic Patients to Their Families

This topic, being the most recent, is the hardest to put into perspective. Dunham has grappled with it in terms of the changes in the urban family (a subject I would like to debate with him at another time), the cost of treatment, the efficacy of the psychotropic drugs, and other interacting variables. In this section, he adduces not only the changing cultural climate, but also the shifting social structure to explain events. Though I would have done the same, I wonder if we are not both looking in the wrong place for insight into this phenomenon.

Early discharge seems to be part and parcel of a decade-long attempt to run down the populations of the hospitals and to remove the locus of treatment to places that are at once smaller than the hospitals and nearer to the patient's usual home. Dunham raises good questions about the assumptions that underlie these programs.

Where do we find evidence that treatment at home is any more effective than treatment in a hospital? The larger question is, why should the nations of the modern industrialized world spend truly vast sums of money to centrifuge, as it were, an enormous service on the basis of so little evidence. I think we have to look to the kinds of explanations offered by historians and political scientists in order to make any sense of it. I think it profitable to attribute at least some of these changes to today's general thrust toward participant democracy, a much larger and more explicitly political movement, with roots in distrust of centralization, size, authority and even in a populist dislike of all expertise. This larger movement is apparently a response to a sense of alienation of citizens from all bureaucracy, especially government. It is a worldwide phenomenon and can be seen not only in the small treatment unit run by egalitarian treatment teams, but also in such things as the refusal of the Norwegians to join the remote and bureaucratized Common Market, and even perhaps in the mammoth Chinese experiment. (Parenthetically, this movement is often said to be a response to the *size* of government, but this seems unlikely for it appears in countries of all sizes.)

Political scientists tell us that the desire for smallness and direct participation on the one hand is in tension with the desire for universalistic standards of performance on the other. This tension results in cycles of demand for decentralization and participation, which are followed by disillusionment with inefficiency and parochialism, leading to demands for centralization, specialization, and efficiency, which in turn are followed by alienation and a demand for participation. They remind us that F. D. Roosevelt's many moves toward centralization were in part a response to the ineffectuality of agencies trying to cope with the depression when they were bogged down in idiosyncratic local practices, nepotism, and lack of expertise.

If the enthusiasm for treatment in the community is indeed part of some larger cyclic process, we might expect to see a re-emergence of enthusiasm for treatment in hospitals staffed with experts. It must be hoped that if that does happen, there will be someone to raise awkward questions about what is going on.

CONCLUSION

We are all in Warren Dunham's debt. Throughout his long career, he has acted out for us a most difficult double role. He has maintained just the right detachment and distance from his subjects to enable him to pursue a most fruitful line of scholarly work in his own field, while making most salutary critical contributions to the field of psychiatry. Those who have never tried this trick have no idea how difficult it is. This book stands as a reminder that just as we are all social scientists, so we are all citizens.

Running through these essays are consistent themes and persistent questions. The questions reflect the doubts of a rational man responding to non-rational enthusiams and irrational claims, but they are never strident and never unkind; they are asked with skepticism and tolerance, which for some of us are two of the characteristics most necessary for civilization.

REFERENCES

1. Robert E. L. Faris, *Chicago Sociology, 1920–1932* (San Francisco: Chandler, 1967).
2. A. Stanton, and M. Schwartz *The Mental Hospital* (New York: Basic Books, 1954).
3. J. Cumming, and E. Cumming, *Ego and Milieu* (New York: Atherton, 1962).
4. E. Cumming, " 'Therapeutic Community' and 'Milieu Therapy' Strategies Can Be Distinguished," *International Journal of Psychiatry*, 7 (April 1969):204–208.
5. E. Cumming, and J. Cumming, "Some Questions on Community Care," *Canada's Mental Health*, XIII (November–December 1965):7–12.
6. R. Glasscote, J. N. Sussex, E. Cumming, and L. H. Smith, *The Community Mental Health Center, an Interim Appraisal* (Washington, D.C.: Joint Information Service of APA and NAMH, 1969): p. 43.
7. William J. Goode, "The Protection of the Inept," *American Sociological Review*, 32 (February 1967): 5–19.
8. T. J. Scheff, "The Labeling Theory of Mental Illness," *American Sociological Review*, 39 (June 1974):444–452.
9. L. S. Kubie, "The Retreat from Patients," *Archives of General Psychiatry*, 24 (February 1971):98–106.
10. Barbara Wootten, *Social Science and Social Pathology* (London: Macmillan, 1959); "Social Psychiatry and Psychotherapy: A Layman's

Comments on Contemporary Developments," In Zubin and Dreyhan (Eds.), *Social Psychiatry* (New York and London: Grune and Stratton, 1967).

INDEX

245

as an etiological force, 30
home, 199
hospital, 207, 211
ideal, 30
and incidence of mental disturbances, 82
in initiating change in state hospitals, 46
local, 209, 211
and mental patients, 66, 81, 83-
84, 95, 112, 187, 199, 216,
219, 221
and mental hospital isolation,
38-39, 77, 195
and mental hospital location, 38
mythical American, 86-87
natural, 170, 173
nature of, 153, 154
organization, 29, 30, 103
outside, 207
pathology of, 104
as a patient, 102, 103, 104
planned, 170, 173
and prevention of mental illness,
105
problems of, 115
professional, 239
protection of, 220
and psychiatrists, 98-101, 129,
140
and rejection of problem personalities, 56
and schizophrenics, 162, 163
social dysfunction of, 128
support, 197
therapeutic, 117, 205, 214, 233
traditional, 170
as a treatment center, 30, 80,
106, 109
urban, 84, 95, 166
Community medicine, 20
Community mental health, 71, 72, 94
Community mental health centers,
71-91, 189, 205, 220
attempt of, 150
in a changing population, 88
and chronic mental illness, 163,
215-17, 224, 234, 236
and community psychiatry, 28, 198
emergence of, 9, 27, 204

factors implementing establishment of, 78-79
first, 196
ideal organization of, 75-77
integration with existing facilities, 85, 197
preventive role of, 81
and psychiatrists, 197
and rehabilitation, 235
and results of treatments, 77-78
rise of, 9, 94
and shift of locus of mental patients, 84, 223
and shift of professional roles,
86
studies of, 72
sociological problems of, 84
unrealistic attitudes towards, 86
urban, 84-85, 88
Community planning, 140
Community psychiatry, 14, 93-
110, 125, 129, 203, 204,
205, 221, 223, 238
acceptance of, 21
action of, 220
and behavior, 136
and clinical psychiatry, 126
and the community, 105, 155
and community mental health
centers, 28
and the definition of mental illness, 114
development of, 29, 117, 212,
213
direction of, 207, 210
duration of, 98
emergence of, 20, 27, 118, 189
implications of, 30, 153, 155,
158
nature of, 94, 96, 97, 143, 149,
151, 198
and national mental health program, 9
need for, 150, 152
preventive function of, 107
as a psychiatric specialty, 93,
96, 111, 150
and psychiatrists, 120
training in, 224
Community psychology, 20

of orientation, 168
of procreation, 168
and the psychiatrist, 98
of the schizophrenic, 162, 163,
165, 167, 169, 171, 172, 173
suburban, 164
Far East, 210
Faris, R. E. L., 12, 13, 230, 243
Finland, 197
Forster, E. F. B., 145
Fort Logan Mental Health Center,
216, 217, 221, 223, 224
Fox, Renee C., 91
Frank, J. D., 41
Frank, Lawrence, 159
Freeman, H. E., 72, 89, 91, 169,
173, 175, 176
Freud, Sigmund, 8, 55

Geriatrics, 95
Gilmore, H., 69
Glasscote, R., 243
Goffman, E., 169, 175
Goldhamer, H., 110, 122, 145
Goldston, W. E., 122
Goode, William J., 243
Gordon, J. E., 123, 188
Gottlieb, Jacques, 175
Greenblat, M., 91
Group for the Advancement of
Psychiatry, 126
Gruenberg, Ernest M., 167, 168,
175, 201
Gumplowicz, Ludwig, 154, 159

Hagar, L., 227
Halfway houses, 180, 223
Halleck, S. L., 23
Heart disease, 209
Herz, Marvin, 21
Hippie movement, 152
Hoch, Paul, 113, 123
Homeostasis, failure of, 209
Horney, Karen, 159
Hospitals, psychiatric wards, 72
Hospital release policy, 189
Hughes, J. M., 201
Human nature, 83
Hyde, R. W., 50

Ideology, 231

Institution, 98
psychiatric, 67
societal, 83, 100, 136, 163, 190
Institutional structures, 129
Insulin coma, 206
Interview
office, 207
therapeutic, 207

Jacks, I., 145
Jahoda, M., 179, 188
Job training, 210
Joint Commission on Mental Illness
and Health, 117, 124, 178, 182,
185, 186, 188
Jones, Ernest, 8
Jones, Maxwell, 18, 27, 50, 61, 68,
116, 123, 226, 227, 228, 232

Kennedy, John F., 26, 28, 32, 116,
124
Kent, 210
Kincheloe, M., 227
Kobrin, S., 106, 107, 108, 122
Kraus, James Israel, 158

Labelling theory, 238
Labour market, 208
Laing, R. D., 10, 11, 169, 175
Lawson, F. S., 72, 89
Lefton, M., 176
Leighton, A., 146, 201
Levi, Lennart, 201
Levinson, P., 91
Lewis, Aubrey, 206, 208
Lin, T., 145, 147
Looseley, E. W., 174
Lowinger, Paul, 175

Manhattan, 179
Marsh, L. C., 18, 23
Marshall, A., 110, 122, 145
Marx, Karl, 11
Massachusetts, 219, 220, 221
Maudsley Hospital, 206, 210
Mayo, Julia A., 90
Mechanic, David, 188
Menninger, W. C., 23, 115, 123, 177,
188
Mental deficiency, 8, 17, 95, 117,
135, 181

248

Mental hospital, see also State Hospital
   behavior of patients in, 40
   community based, 97, 196
   and community mental health centers, 196
   failure of, 191
   as an ineffective therapeutic instrument, 79
   and models, 170
   orientation courses, 48
   resident, 48
   and schizophrenia, 162
   "snakepit image," 222
   socialization program, 49
   sociological studies of, 54, 78-79
   and the superintendent, 44
   work programs in, 48
Mental hygiene, 19
Mental illness, see also Character disorders, Neuroses, Psychoses
   schizophrenia, 8, 125, 136, 138
   in the community, 105, 117, 119, 180
   and community psychiatry, 130, 213
   coping with, 143, 171
   and culture, 17, 157, 192
   definition of, 7
   denial of, 166
   and family, 101, 192
   hospitalization for, 116
   and mental health policy, 22
   nature of, 10, 104, 196
   origin of, 192
   physiological and genetic factors of, 135, 186
   prevention of, 100, 131-34, 152, 158
   public health problem of, 46
   rate of, 141
   and social action, 180, 187, 198
   social model of, 11
   social prejudice of, 10
   surveys of, 95, 111, 112, 178, 181, 182
   treatment of, 200, 206, 207
   widening definition of, 20, 93, 111, 112, 114, 119, 121, 138, 152, 153, 181
Merton, R. K., 102, 122

Milieu
   social, 102, 103
   subcultural, 111
   therapeutic, 18, 189, 194, 195
Miller, Daniel R., 164, 174
Mill Hill Emergency Hospital, 209, 210
Minnesota, 97
Mitchell, Weir, 8
Model
   behavioral, 169, 170
   of caring parents, 206
   community mental health care, 204
   community mental health center, 73
   criminal, 107
   exploratory, 204
   hedonic, 169, 170
   imprisonment, 169, 170
   medical, 10, 14, 16, 22, 169, 170, 185, 189, 237, 238
   of mental illness, 169
   natural science, 129
   natural system, 127
   rational, 127, 134
   social, 10, 11, 151
   social-ecological, 128
   social system, 127
   state hospital, 223
   theoretical, 127
   therapeutic community, 214
Morale, staff, 195, 213
Myerson, Abraham, 19, 23, 201

National Institute of Mental Health, 95, 96, 204
National Mental Health Act, 46, 115, 178, 189
Nazi Germany, 193
Netherlands, 19, 51
Neuroses, 16, 82, 95, 101, 137, 157, 181, 192, 235
   cardiac, 207
New York City, 167
New York State, 113, 220
Nicol, Susan, 175
Nightingale, Florence, 79
Night hospitals, 72, 94, 97, 116, 163, 180
Norway, 19, 72

250

social, 168, 211
social psychiatry, 126
vocational, 211

Roosevelt, F. D., 241
Rousseau, J., 11, 193
Rowland, H., 68
Rubie, L. S., 243

St. Louis, 164
San Jose, California, 218
Santa Clara County Aftercare Services, 213
Santayana, G., 68
Scheff, T. J., 238, 243
Schiff, J., 228
Schizophrenia, 234
  cure of, 174, 186
  incidence of, 134, 138, 183
  Laing interpretation of, 10
  reduction of, 82, 135
  and social class, 13
  survey of, 112
  treatment of, 21, 206, 214, 215
Schofield, W., 23
Schwartz, M., 32, 42, 68, 91, 116, 123, 146, 243
Scotland, 214, 221, 222
Seeley, J., 165, 174
Self-image, 213
Sex offenders, 111
Skellern, E., 68
Simmons, O. G., 91, 169, 175, 176
Sims, R., 174
Smith, L. H., 243
Social action, 151, 179, 187
  in mental health, 180
Social-breakdown syndrome, 167, 168
Social causation, 156, 233
Social change, 101, 102, 171, 198
  swiftness of, 167
Social control, 121, 237
  agent of, 237
  mechanisms of, 151
Social engineering, 128, 206
Social interaction, 206
Social learning, 206, 213
Social organization, 205
Social sciences, 129, 142, 163

Social situation, 52, 54-57, 59
  institutional, 56
  ward, 61
Social structure, 210, 231
Socialization, 17
Society, 54
  hospital, 207, 208
Sociology, 127, 150
  of knowledge, 171
  nature of, 154
Solomon, H. C., 50
South Africa, 193
Spectorsky, A. C., 174
Srole, L., 123, 188
Stanton, A., 32, 42, 68, 91, 116, 123, 146, 243
State Hospital, see also Mental hospital
  attitudes in, 42
  authoritarian, 43
  changes in, 46
  cultural system of, 45
  and community health programs, 73
  democratic, 43
  industrial units, 72
  isolation of, 39
  as a model, 47
  number of patients in, 114
  reorganization of, 86, 95, 180
  role of, 94
  size of, 38
  traditional, 75, 77, 117
Stromgren, Erik, 72, 89
Strotzka, Hans, 72, 90
Subcultures, 54, 58, 64, 102, 170
  institutional, 33
Sussex, J. N., 243
Swanson, Guy E., 164, 174
System
  authority, 206
  family, 215
  open, 214, 222, 223, 225, 226
  social, 224, 231
Szasz, T. S., 123

Theory
  communication, 205
  learning, 205
  systems, 205, 206, 213

251